THE WIT & WISDOM OF
Dr Mahathir Mohamad

EDITORIAL DIRECTOR
Martin Cross

EDITORIAL CONSULTANT
Philip Mathews

ASSISTANT EDITORS
Ian Ting Sze Lim • Reba Koleth

RESEARCHERS
Karmaljeet Kaur Kaulsay • Joane Sharmila

DESIGNER
Vani Nadaraju

PRODUCTION MANAGER
Sin Kam Cheong

PUBLISHED BY
Editions Didier Millet Sdn Bhd
25 Jalan Pudu Lama
50200 Kuala Lumpur
Malaysia

www.edmbooks.com

ISBN: 978-967-10617-6-3

Jacket image: Alvin Wong

First published in 2014

Printed by Tien Wah Press, Singapore

THE WIT & WISDOM OF
Dr Mahathir Mohamad

CONTENTS

PUBLISHER'S NOTE

Dr Mahathir Mohamad served as prime minister of Malaysia for 22 years. He provided visionary leadership to the nation and, on the international stage, he was a commanding voice for the rights and dignity of the developing world who ably articulated Malaysia's point of view in the global arena.

A fervent nationalist, Mahathir was shaped by his strict upbringing and his experiences during the Japanese Occupation and under the British colonial administration. After the war he joined the newly formed United Malays National Organisation (UMNO) and, while studying at medical college, was often published in newspapers under the pseudonym 'Che Det'. He went on to qualify and practise as a medical doctor before becoming an MP in 1964. After the 13 May 1969 riots, Mahathir criticised the UMNO leadership and was expelled from the party as a result. During this period of political exile, he wrote his seminal *The Malay Dilemma* in which he outlined his views on the plight of the Malays. In 1972 he was invited back into UMNO and was re-elected as an MP in 1974. He then rose inexorably from minister to deputy prime minister before reaching Malaysia's highest political office in 1981.

As prime minister, Mahathir was at the forefront of the nation's economic development. He initiated key policies including the Malaysia Incorporated concept of public–private cooperation and the Look East policy to emulate the work ethic of successful Asian countries, particularly Japan and Korea. These policies fuelled his drive towards Vision 2020, his ideal of making Malaysia a developed nation by 2020.

It was under Mahathir's leadership that Malaysia secured its place in the global arena. In particular, when his strong self-belief showed through during the Asian Financial Crisis of 1997–98 as he withstood strong international pressure and introduced policies which flew in the face of orthodox economic dogma at that time. His stand was ultimately vindicated.

Dr Mahathir stepped down as prime minister in 2003, but has continued to remain in the public eye and to contribute to public debate through his widely read blog and regular public appearances and speeches. This collection of his quotations includes insights into Mahathir's strong views and perspectives on many facets of Malaysia and a wide range of broader issues. The quotations have for the most part been selected from Dr Mahathir's public speeches and statements, which have been collected at the Perdana Leadership Foundation in Putrajaya.

ON MALAYSIA

Under the guidance of my illustrious predecessors, we have established a stable democratic government, a sound economy and the basis of an efficient national infrastructure. We are well endowed with natural resources, we are spared the horrors of some of the natural disasters that afflict some of our close neighbours; and our people, whatever their race, attach great importance to high spiritual and religious values. We, therefore, have very solid grounds for optimism for the future.

National Seminar on Productivity, Kuala Lumpur, 1982

Malaysia is a developing country with a multiracial population. Although we can be proud of the development we have achieved since our independence 26 years ago, we are still far behind when compared with the developed countries. We do not just wish for wealth, but we realise that a nation and a people that is weak and backward will not be respected. We have to acquire all forms of knowledge that is now possessed by the developed nations in order to safeguard our honour and integrity. It is only when we have attained their level of development that we will be able to hold our own and not be pushed around and bullied. Only those without honour are willing to let their nation be belittled. Our principal hope and aim is to safeguard the sovereignty of this nation and the honour of its people.

Launch of Leadership by Example Campaign, Kuala Lumpur, 1983

Not being known in America is actually a good thing – it means that we are peaceful and stable. So I am not unduly worried about Malaysia not being famous although a lot of other Malaysians feel hurt when they are asked whether Malaysia is in China or Africa. So long as the business community knows Malaysia, that is all that really matters.

Luncheon hosted by Asia Society, Far East American Business Council
and ASEAN–American Trade Council, New York, 1984

While I am sure that you all know where I am from, Malaysia is not the best-known country in America. Everyone knows Thailand because of 'The King and I'; Singapore because Bob Hope and Bing Crosby took the 'Road to Singapore', Indonesia because you had trouble with Sukarno and the Philippines because you once ruled it. But Malaysia is a new country and has not done those things so loved by the sensationalist Western press. Head-hunting went out of fashion in the early part of this century and the biggest tree is no longer reserved for the prime minister as his house.

Luncheon hosted by Asia Society, Far East American Business Council
and ASEAN–American Trade Council, New York, 1984

Malaysia has fully committed itself to the pursuit of excellence. In the last five years we have critically examined all the things that we have been doing or which we have taken for granted. We have questioned old policies and approaches. We have even assaulted many administrative and management methods that have been considered sacred. At least the government has.

World Management Conference, Kuala Lumpur, 1985

Being a democratic country, Malaysia has the usual quota of malcontents who will tell you that all is not well with this country. We are liberal and they will no doubt be speaking to you in this forum and outside. For the sake of impressing, they have to exaggerate and suggest dark things. The more interesting tales will be told unofficially outside.

EMF Foundation Round Table, Kuala Lumpur, 1986

Malaysia is a new country that came into being without the usual big bang. Until 1963 we were known as Malaya. Indeed some American writers still refer to us as Malaya. For us it is logical to rename the country Malaysia when the states of Sarawak, Sabah and Singapore joined the federation. But maybe it is not so logical to distant foreigners. After all, Himalaya is in India. Couldn't Malaysia be somewhere between China and India, or Africa which has Malawi and Mali? *American International Group Investment Seminar, Kuala Lumpur, 1986*

Let me say something about Malaysia. We are what we are partly because of the contribution by the British. I will not pretend that there was such a country as Malaysia before the British came. We were separate small Malay Sultanates which had a tendency to break up into smaller states because the Sultans gave away chunks of land which then became Malay states. The British created Malaya and created the preconditions for Malaysia.

Dinner hosted by British-Malaysian Society, London, 1987

৵

To those of you from overseas, I bid you all a warm welcome, particularly those visiting Malaysia for the first time. I hope the beauty of our land and the friendliness of our people will make you feel that the visit has been worthwhile. The real test lies in the future – on whether you will be back again, to visit and to invest.

World Economic Forum National Meeting on Malaysia, Kuala Lumpur, 1989

৵

Despite its multiracial composition and presumed tendency towards violent conflicts, Malaysia has been so politically stable that it has made very good economic progress throughout the 33 years of its independence.

International Chinese Newspapers Convention, Kuala Lumpur, 1990

৵

We were a domino, ready to fall to the communists. We are now a dynamo.

Institute of Strategic and International Studies, Kuala Lumpur, 1993

৵

Malaysia is a developing third-world country. We should, according to the stereotypical western concept of a third-world country, be politically unstable, administratively incompetent and economically depressed. But we are not quite typical. We have actually made progress. We are quite stable despite a multiracial time-bomb we inherited from our colonial past. We are fairly competent in the running of our affairs, such is our progress that we actually contemplated building buildings which should be the preserve of our better. And we dare to speak our minds.

United Nations General Assembly, New York, 1993

We should make Malaysia the gateway for products and services from other parts of the world to the countries in this region. In competing for the global market, we have to ensure that our management practices are up to the highest standards and we must uncompromisingly benchmark ourselves against the world's best.

Last speech as Prime Minister in Dewan Rakyat, Kuala Lumpur, 2003

৯৯

Although Malaysia is not a communist country, it has been willing to use methods originating from communist or capitalist countries. Malaysia has no ideology. It merely wants to prosper its people and the country as a whole. Malaysia is simply pragmatic, accepting and doing what would produce results, irrespective of ideologies.

Global Competitive Forum, Riyadh, Saudi Arabia, 2009

ON MALAYSIANS

Last year, I said that the recession was a godsend. The recession can be regarded as an opportunity for us to toughen ourselves and to be more productive. The recession has enabled our drive for higher productivity to be off to a good start. More Malaysians, if not all of them, are cultivating the spirit of hard work and diligence.

National Chamber of Commerce and Industry, Kuala Lumpur, 1983

৯

We must prove that we can develop our country ourselves without depending on others. And I am confident we can do this if we acquire efficiency in all our endeavours.

Lawas, Sarawak, 1983

৯

Malaysians are by nature sentimental, and they value friendship and common history even though some episodes may not be palatable to them.

Dinner in honour of Margaret Thatcher, Kuala Lumpur, 1985

৯

It is very important we have close and cordial ties as one big family of Malaysians and we will not lose anything by doing so.

National Family Day, Kuala Lumpur, 1990

৯

If we want a better life, each Malaysian should be able to replace two or three expatriates. Our income will surely also be doubled.

MIC General Assembly, Kuala Lumpur, 1996

৯

We are culturally not Europeans, we cannot make their solutions, their systems and their mindsets work for us.

Asia Human Resource Development Conference, Jakarta, 2006

The good thing about Malaysians is that they are peaceful people who do not like violence. If they do not like a leader, they do not resort to exploding bombs and killing the leader. They will tolerate the leader and hope for the best. I think leaders in Malaysia should be happy as they do not have to worry about being assassinated. I have survived 83 years as a leader. But I suppose in some other countries if I were driven around standing in an open car, I might have to sit down very quickly.

Perdana Discourse Series 7, Perdana Leadership Foundation, Putrajaya, 2008

❧

It is time the silent majority stop being silent. It is time to speak up and be counted. If we love our country we must not allow crooks and charlatans to rape and steal it from us. It is ours, this country of many races and religions. We must stand together, we the concerned Malaysians, and defend our heritage.

Chedet.cc blog, 2008

❧

Now what would be a Bangsa Malaysia? I believe that we will not be like Switzerland or America. I don't think we would be successful in getting everybody to use Bahasa Malaysia as their home language. At home, they will still speak their own dialect or language, but at least they should all be able to speak the national language fluently. That is what they should do. They should feel that they are of the same race and people living in the same country, Malaysia, therefore they should be Bangsa Malaysia. To a certain extent, they do feel that. Whenever I go abroad, I meet many Malaysians and they come to me and say, 'we are Malaysians'. They don't tell me they are Chinese or Indian Malaysians; although it is obvious they are, and most certainly Malays do not say we are Malay Malaysians. They are all Malaysians when they are abroad.

Perdana Discourse Series 8, Perdana Leadership Foundation, Putrajaya, 2008

❧

We Malaysians can do what others can do.

Chedet.cc blog, 2012

ON COLONIALISM
AND IMPERIALISM

The arrival of the Portuguese, the Dutch and finally the British gave this trend the final push. It must be remembered that the Europeans came out East not to conquer but to trade. In the quest of trade, however, they were prepared to do anything. They conquered and they plundered. They made treaties and they broke them. They were in fact unscrupulous. *The Malay Dilemma, 1970*

ଈ

The age of empires and imperial powers is practically over. But the world has not as yet become a better place for the previously colonised. There are many reasons for this, and among them is the banding together of the rich nations in order to maintain economic dominance, which some say is actually a form of imperialism. We, in Malaysia, are very much affected by this. As a nation we have tried to live within the rules, formal and informal, which govern the economic relations between nations. We have even refrained from nationalising industries set up during colonial days, which were engaged in literally extracting wealth from our country for foreigners who frequently do not even know where Malaysia is, much less care for the well-being of its people.

United Nations General Assembly, New York, 1982

ଈ

We have taken pains to preserve the relics of history. In the heart of Kuala Lumpur, for example, we have preserved that typically English scene consisting of a cricket ground, a club (in mock Tudor) and a church. We preserve all these not because of our sentimentality. The world is now not very much moved by sentiments. We preserve them as reminders of our past, so that Malaysians will not forget that they were once colonised by various European powers. If they do not wish to be colonised again, in whatever form, they must learn to manage their affairs better.

Dinner in honour of Margaret Thatcher, Kuala Lumpur, 1985

Although our past has been linked with many countries in the East and the West, it is with Britain that the association is longest. Britain gave us a Malaysian identity where once there was identification only with the little states where we lived. Britain also inspired our system of government and left the rudiments of an administration which we have built up with great enthusiasm, although perhaps unwisely.

Dinner in honour of Margaret Thatcher, Kuala Lumpur, 1985

&

A case can be made that we have already moved into a period of 'soft imperialism' where the foundations of a nation's power are more likely to rest on brains rather than brawn, on the creativity, energy and talent of its people rather than on the size of its population and the extent of its territory. Increasingly, it can be argued, national prosperity and political power will hinge not on the lands that an army can conquer and the number of people that a nation can subjugate but on the degree of penetration of markets, the extent to which other peoples are reliant on one's financial flows, technology and domestic market, the extent to which they are dependent on the products that one can provide and the services that one can render.

Asia-Pacific Roundtable, Kuala Lumpur, 1989

&

Soft imperialism too can be perverted by the desire for pomp and glory, and by the will to dominate and dictate. But conducted in an enlightened and therefore sustainable manner, this soft imperialism is not a zero-sum game. Indeed, it is a process that promises a wealth of mutual benefit – because the interest of the expansionist power is inherently and critically tied to the comprehensive prosperity of the countries which are targets. If I am right and what we will see in the years ahead are increasing examples of economic expansionism and decreasing attempts at military expansionism, then we can expect much more of our future to be determined by the trading state rather than by the garrison and the military state.

Asia-Pacific Roundtable, Kuala Lumpur, 1989

When Sukarno, a contemporary of Pandit Nehru, coined the word 'neocolonialism', we thought he was being rhetorical. Now we know he knew better. What we are experiencing now is indeed a new form of colonialism, more insidious than open colonialism.

Conferment of the Jawaharlal Nehru Award, New Delhi, 1996

The 1,000 years that we leave behind us have seen some of the worst examples of men's exploitation and oppression of men. We have seen the colonisation of many nations and the exploitation of their economic wealth by and for a few nations. We have seen the destruction of human souls through slavery and bondage, through genocides and wars that mock the claim that man is at the apex of God's creatures. We have seen the greed of selfish and powerful men destroying the hard-earned wealth of nations, and their hard-working people. All this and more will be part of the baggage of history that we will carry into the new century and millennium.

Africa–Asia Business Forum, Kuala Lumpur, 1999

During the second half of the 20th century, competition for influence between the Western Bloc and Communist Russia led to the freeing of the Asian colonies of the European powers. The reason given for this generosity on the part of the European colonial powers was humanitarian. It was wrong, it seems, for people to colonise other people and other countries. But the true reason was fear that the colonial people would side with the other bloc. The desire to dominate remains and it was a matter of time before this desire manifests itself again.

Asia Society Gala Forum, Hong Kong, 2000

One of the central truths about our times is that the second great age of colonialism is already upon us. This may be fine and dandy for the perpetrators and the beneficiaries. It is not so fine and dandy for the victims and the potential victims. For Malaysia, I say that 450 years of colonialism is enough. Malaysia must be free. We must be free to decide our future for ourselves.

World Economic Development Congress, Kuala Lumpur, 2001

We, the small nations, have much to be grateful for. From being the colonies of the Europeans, we are now independent and we are granted membership of the United Nations with the right to speak, albeit with proper restraint and decorum at this august assembly. And as independent nations, we believe we have a right to manage our internal affairs ourselves without foreign interference.
United Nations General Assembly, New York, 2003

ॐ

History has a way of repeating itself. The giant corporations and banks which belong to the rich western countries can behave like the East India Companies of the past. From merely demanding unfettered trade, they can go on to dominate and control the governments of the countries which had been opened to them. The end result will not be much different from the colonisation which had followed trading by the European trading companies of the past. Then the struggle for independence can begin all over again.
Asia-Pacific Parliamentary Forum, Kuala Lumpur, 2003

ॐ

We all carry the baggage of history. But we would willingly leave them behind if it were not for the fact that history has a nasty habit of repeating itself. Today we are seeing the resurgence of European imperialism. At first we thought the colonisation would be virtual. Merely by economic strangulation and financial emasculation, the newly independent countries could be brought to their knees, begging to be recolonised in other forms. But today we are actually faced by the old physical occupation by foreign forces. Puppet regimes are installed dancing as puppets do.
United Nations General Assembly, New York, 2003

ॐ

The former colonies of the Europeans may have gained independence in the legal sense. But many are not truly independent. Politically and economically they remain no better than colonies. For a time their borders are respected. But then came new ideas about a globalised world, a world without borders. How can a country be independent if its borders are not sacred, if anyone can cross its borders freely and do anything he likes within the country?
Asia-Pacific Parliamentary Forum, Kuala Lumpur, 2003

Malaysia is leery of any proposal for improving trade. It was trade with the Europeans that led to us being conquered and colonised. We had no problem with the traders from Arabia, India and China. But with the Europeans, we had any number of problems. We therefore wonder whether the present proposals for globalisation and free trade will not again bring problems for us, bring back colonisation of some kind, or at the very least hegemonise us.

Regional Geo Economic Forum, Zagreb, Croatia, 2004

જી

For centuries, the mindsets of the colonial people were shaped and determined. To this day, many believe that unless they adopt European ways and standards, European practices, they would not succeed.

Asia Human Resource Development Congress, Jakarta, 2006

જી

If our country remains poor and weak, we would not be truly independent. Necolonialism is not a fancy term coined by President Sukarno. It is real. We feel it as we come under the control of agencies owned by our former colonial masters. Our struggle for independence is not over yet. It will only be over after we become a fully developed country.

Asia Human Resource Development Congress, Jakarta, 2006

જી

I would not be wrong if I say that the mess we are in today has its origins in the western imperialism of the past. During the heyday of colonialism, they had no compunction about drawing borders which divided people, changing demography by moving large numbers of people to occupy other people's land, and when they had to give up their empires, time bombs were left everywhere: racial, religious, economic, financial and military time bombs. They then insisted on the new states practising democracy even though they themselves had imposed authoritarian rules when they were occupying their colonies.

Stability and Justice and Rights of Al-Quds and Palestine, Kuala Lumpur, 2010

ON THE MALAY RULERS

Before the people toppled the Rulers and the monarchy system, as has already happened in several countries, the government had to act quickly to save the monarchy system through constitutional amendments to place the Rulers in the rightful place.

Karachi, Pakistan 1993

❧

Some Rulers misbehaved even more after criticisms behind closed doors.

Karachi, Pakistan 1993

❧

The British interpreted protection as colonisation, however the Rulers were happy enough to sign the treaties without knowing fully the implications as long as they got a good life. They were given political pensions, provided with palaces, Rolls-Royces and yellow umbrellas. These were very important things to them. However, the decision they made was based on improper, incorrect or incomplete information. If they had known what the British were like, I think they would have hesitated.

Perdana Leadership Foundation, Putrajaya, 2007

❧

Despite the invasion by the Europeans, the Malay Rulers still considered themselves as vassal states, not colonies. When they initially entered into a relationship with the British, they thought they were becoming vassal states of the British. They mistakenly thought that they could send gold and silver flowers in return for autonomy, to rule their states as they see fit with minimal advice from the British. Unfortunately the British had other ideas. Once they established themselves, they treated the Malay States as colonies over which they exerted their rule and left the local Rulers without any authority. The local Rulers were told not to be involved in the running of their states and they were compensated in the form of allowances, palaces to live in, and continuation of royal traditions and practices.

Perdana Leadership Foundation, Putrajaya, 2008

Can the King dismiss the prime minister? The answer is 'no' if the political framework is that of constitutional monarchy and there are no express provisions in the Constitution. Additionally, constitutional conventions provide no precedent for the exercise of such a power. The Malaysian Constitution, Article 40, expressly provides that the Yang di-Pertuan Agong shall act on advice and, by Article 40(2), may act in his discretion in the performance of the following functions, that is to say: the appointment of a prime minister; the withholding of consent to a request for the dissolution of Parliament; the requisition of a meeting of the Conference of Rulers concerned solely with the privileges, position, honours and dignities of their Royal Highnesses, and any action at such meeting; and in any other cases mentioned in this Constitution. But the relevant article that will close the debate on whether the Agong can dismiss the prime minister is contained in Article 43(5) of the Constitution. Subject to clause (4), ministers other than the prime minister shall hold office during the pleasure of the Yang di-Pertuan Agong, unless the appointment of any minister shall be revoked by the Yang di-Pertuan Agong on the advice of the prime minister but any minister may resign his office. But, since the prime minister does not hold office at the pleasure of the Yang di-Pertuan Agong, it must follow that he cannot be dismissed by the King, but he has to resign from office if he fails to command the majority of the members in the House of Representatives.

Chedet.cc blog, 2009

❧

Malaysians as a whole respect and honour the Malay Rulers. Usually they avoid criticisms of royalty. Even the government would try to cover up serious misdemeanours by the Sultans. The occasions when the government had to do this were few and far between, but certainly some involved serious cases.

A Doctor in the House, 2011

ON DEMOCRACY

Let me now turn to the really big one: the constant criticism that the Third World does not practise democracy and the constant pressure for all of us to adopt the system of 'participatory democracy'. Let me state quite categorically that I am in favour of democracy, of government of the people, by the people, for the people. At the same time, I believe that in practice, each nation must seek its own path to democracy. Neither the British form of democracy nor the American form of democracy – two distinct and different forms of democracy – can be exported whole and installed, ready-made, in a very large number of countries. What a hue and cry there would be in Britain were the Americans to force their particular brand down British throats. What a big shake-out and a big shoo-in at the top of the civil service every time a new president is elected? Judges to be chosen by the people? Non-members of the Commons to be chosen as ministers of the Crown? A clear division of powers between the executive and the legislature? An end to party discipline? Heavens.

Trinity College, Oxford, 1985

ॐ

Democracy must confer a freedom of choice. No one has a monopoly on the democratic type that everyone should have. Certainly, no one should force his own choice and interpretation on someone else. While harsh and even violent methods may be used to force dictatorship to yield to democratic forces, it would be tragic if a working, prosperous democratic nation is destroyed because some self-appointed democrat felt it was not democratic enough. This 'holier than thou' attitude is out of tune with modern mores.

United Nations General Assembly, New York, 1988

ॐ

Democracy is being preached by the liberal democrats of the West with religious fervour. Everyone must accept liberal democracy or have their countries destabilised, civil war fomented or at the very least [subjected to] economic sanction and vilification by the media.

Non-Aligned Movement, Belgrade, Yugoslavia, 1989

Countries which for thousands of years had only known authoritarian rule cannot become democratic overnight. Sudden freedom will result in disruptions, which in turn will retard the progress towards a more liberal and open society. The liberal democrats of the West should cease trying to force the pace.   *Non-Aligned Movement, Belgrade, Yugoslavia, 1989*

≈▲·

Democracy must not be an end in itself. It must remain a means to an end – the installation of good governments in the true sense of the word. Making a religion of democracy, accepting everything that is done in its name unquestioningly will only destroy the faith in the efficacy of the system. Forcing it down the throats of people who are not ready for it will not do any good either.

International Conference on the ASEAN Countries and the World Economy, Bali, 1991

≈▲·

People who sell democracy in the world must be prepared to provide some after-sale service to keep democracy alive.

Commonwealth Summit Talk, Limassol, Cyprus, 1993

≈▲·

Democracy is for our own good, but we should not be sacrificed for the sake of democracy. Once again, do not be hoodwinked by the West. Do not be too obsessed with their ideologies without considering the consequences. Democracy is good but its benefits are more important. We practise democracy because of promises of its goodness but we should not sacrifice ourselves and the good cause that we have struggled for due to being obsessed with democracy, especially the liberal Western democracy.

UMNO General Assembly, Kuala Lumpur, 2000

≈▲·

Democracy is meant to serve us, not we to serve democracy.

Malaysia in the New Millennium Conference, London, 2000

Is it democratic to have the same party returned time and time again? Some say it is not democratic. They say a democratic country must see frequent changes of government. Will the future see such changes? It is possible of course. Many are already saying that we need a change, we need a new government merely for the sake of change.

Malaysia in the New Millennium conference, London, 2000

&

Changing government may be considered democratic but it is very disruptive. It affects a country's development adversely. Again we have to consider whether we want democracy for its sake or we want democracy for the good that it can deliver. *Malaysia in the New Millennium Conference, London,* 2000

&

Democracy implies the upholding of the rights of the majority. This must necessarily be negated if the norms of the majority can be totally disregarded by individuals. One cannot help feeling that in this matter the world is very confused, insisting on the upholding of values which are totally incompatible. Yet woe betide those who try to practise the rights of the majority as implied by democracy. Now even the propagation of democracy itself is undemocratic. Democracy means free choice. When there were autocratic rulers, the democrats struggled for free choice, i.e. free choice of the systems of government including choosing democracy. But now no one is allowed to choose anything except democracy.

World Fellowship of Buddhists Conference, Shah Alam, 2002

&

Clearly it is not the system that counts, it is the practitioners of the system. A benevolent and caring autocrat can do wonders to develop a nation. On the other hand, a democracy with numerous bickering political parties, none of which are big enough to provide a strong government, all of which are bent on disruptions of all kinds in order to bring down the incumbent, will also not be stable. The people are supposed to be wise and to choose a government that will be good for them. But the reality is that people are not wise, not even the majority of them.

Non-Aligned Movement's Business South–South Cooperation, Kuala Lumpur, 2003

Elections may not result in the best candidates winning. Bribery, thuggery, badmouthing, religious trickery, nepotism and numerous other unsavoury ways can bring victory to the candidates least suitable to lead a nation.

Ho Rih Hwa Public Lecture Series, Singapore, 2004

Some Asian countries are so fearful that leaders might become dictators that they provide constitutionally one term for each leader. Only a miracle worker of a leader can produce results in one term. It is impossible for a developing country to develop if, every five years, a new policy and plan is launched by a new leader to make a mark for himself. Merely learning about leading a nation, knowing the routines and the procedures would take a year. It would take two years more to formulate and get parliamentary support for the policy, if at all. And the two years that are left are not even enough to launch the plan or policy, much less to see results.

Ho Rih Hwa Public Lecture Series, Singapore, 2004

In Malaysia political campaigns never stop. It goes on from the announcement of the result of the current elections to the time when the campaign for the next elections begins. One party campaigns during communal prayers on Friday and every time there is a communal daily prayer. It goes on from dawn to midnight and beyond, where the party rules. The loudspeakers blare out hatred for the government it is opposed to.

Ho Rih Hwa Public Lecture Series, Singapore, 2004

The right of the worker to go on strike, for example, can be made into a very effective political weapon. Strikes, especially general strikes nationwide, can bring down governments. Perhaps some governments which are perceived to be abusing power and to manipulate elections need to be brought down this way. But unfortunately such a method of bringing down government can be habit-forming. Duly elected governments may not be able to stay the course because of such strikes. When the government is overthrown and a new election brings a new government into power, it too would be brought down by the same means.

G-15 FFCIS Board Meeting, Kuala Lumpur, 2006

Authoritarian rule is risky as abuses are very common. It would require a violent revolution to end such rule. Today the system of choice and the system that is being forcefully promoted is democracy.

G-15 FFCIS Board Meeting, Kuala Lumpur, 2006

ﾂ｣

Now in a democratic system, we presume that the majority of the people know what is best for them. However, this assumption that the majority knows what is good for them may not be always correct. They may have twisted ideas they are a superior race and because they make up the majority, they would choose a government that would represent the majority but be very oppressive to the minority. Therefore, the majority is not always right, but they would be less prone to make mistakes if they were properly informed. But who is going to inform them?

Perdana Discourse Series 6, Perdana Leadership Foundation, Putrajaya, 2007

ﾂ｣

In Malaysia, it is not only information that influences us in making decisions. Sometimes, we make decisions quite blindly based on our race, our religion and our party. I do not care what really happens but this is our party and therefore I must vote for my party, even though I know that the party is doing something wrong. With this kind of mentality, information will not work very well.

Perdana Discourse Series 6, Perdana Leadership Foundation, Putrajaya, 2007

ﾂ｣

Switzerland has decided that Muslim mosques in that country would not be allowed to have minarets. It seems that minarets would overwhelm the Swiss. I wonder what would happen in Malaysia if Hindu temples are not allowed to have statues, for example. I think there would be an explosion. The whole world will condemn us as being undemocratic, not respecting human rights, not upholding religious freedom, etc. But when the Swiss ban minarets (there are only four minarets in the whole of Switzerland) and the French ban headscarves, these are very democratic. Always double standards and, unfortunately, the discrimination is always against Muslims.

Chedet.cc blog, 2009

There is no way a government can please everyone. But still it must try to do so. This it can do if it is committed to upholding justice and fair play. Even the opposition must be given their due. Favouritism and abuses of power have to be avoided. *International Forum, Cairo*, 2011

୬

If there is one thing that we should know about democracy, it is that it is no longer the simple system to enable the citizens to elect their own governments. To it has been added numerous qualifications such as the rule of law, freedoms of speech and of the press, minority rights, the right to form trade unions and to strike and the setting-up of non-governmental organisations, etc. But still the essence of democracy is the right of the people to elect their governments. *International Forum, Cairo*, 2011

୬

People as a whole must understand the workings of democracy. Ultimately, the need is for mindsets and cultural values compatible with democracy. There are of course many other things that have to be in place or need to be done on the path to democracy. These have to be attended to. It may take time. It may fail repeatedly even. But patience would be needed. Just wanting to be democratic is not enough. *International Forum, Cairo*, 2011

୬

Democracy is not an instant formula. It took about 200 years to develop to its present form. Even then it is far from being perfect. After all it is a creation of the human mind. *International Forum, Cairo*, 2011

୬

It is worthwhile noting that even in mature democracies, like the United States for example, assassinations of leaders have taken place. But the reaction is not general violence and a breakdown of law and order. Instead, the government would take legal action to punish the assailants. The people generally reject such attempts to overthrow governments.

International Forum, Cairo, 2011

Democracy will also fail when democratic freedoms are abused. Street demonstrations and general strikes are democratic but, if indulged in without valid reasons, it will undermine stability, economic activities and development of the country. We see this happening in several new democracies. No sooner is a government elected than general strikes and demonstrations would be launched and kept up until proper administration cannot be carried out. The government may fall but the next government elected would face the same problem and would also fail. Democratic freedoms must be used sparingly.   *International Forum, Cairo,* 2011

❧

Everyone should be prepared to give the government enough time to govern the country. If it fails it should be rejected at the next election. In the end it is the maturity of the people that makes democracy work.

International Forum, Cairo, 2011

❧

Democracy itself is often not even democratic. The people, the ordinary citizens, never really govern themselves.   *Chedet.cc blog,* 2012

❧

Regime change may be desirable but it is wrong for the West to force it on people who may not be ready for it. The process must be through education and the slow spread of the principles of democracy and its weaknesses. The focus should be on the next generation, which will be more appreciative of the good points of democracy and understand how it works. The most important point is that some will lose in elections. They must then be patient enough to wait for the next election. A bad government is better than a destabilised government. If the government is really bad, it will not win the next election.   *Chedet.cc blog,* 2013

ON THE BARISAN NASIONAL

When dealing with race relations, the coalition government never fails to consider the views of all races rather than the majority race only as would happen in a multiracial party where one race dominates. The Robin Hood approach of robbing the rich to give to the poor is rejected by the coalition. Instead it tends to nurture the rich so they will contribute to the welfare of the poor through fair taxes. In fact we sometimes reduce taxes if we think that by doing so we can persuade the goose that laid the golden eggs to lay more and bigger eggs. And it worked. In Malaysia today the Chinese are richer than they were before, but the Malays also get a reasonable share of the wealth.

Malaysia in the New Millennium Conference, London, 2000

Dato' Onn [Jaafar], the first president of UMNO, had wanted to open UMNO to non-Malays and make it a multiracial party. The Tunku sensed that neither the Malays nor the other races were ready to ignore their ethnic and cultural origins and accept the leadership of anyone not from their own race. And so he proposed a coalition in which race-based parties could come together to struggle for common causes. This way the bigger race or party would not be able to dominate absolutely. The identity of the minority race or party would not be lost. And if the minority felt that their interests were not being attended to, they could raise the issues in a council where they have the same number of representatives. They felt safer and so they can accommodate the views of other parties and races without fear of losing much of their racial identity and interest. And they could accept the leadership of someone from another race because he is only the first among equals.

Malaysia in the New Millennium Conference, London, 2000

Although the developed countries are against the present Barisan Nasional government and would like to see a change of government in Malaysia, I suspect that they are not going to like a PAS government any more than they do the present government. They will continue to be busy trying to undermine this so-called Muslim government.

Malaysia in the New Millennium Conference, London, 2000

ॐ

The only party which is nearest to being multiracial is the National Front[1]. Although it is a coalition of parties, it functions as a single party with every race in Malaysia represented equally in its central council irrespective of the size of the component. In addition the component parties all use the same symbol during elections. Its policies are accepted by all the component parties, unlike the Pakatan where each party has its own objectives and policies. The BN has a distinct leader acknowledged by every party and the governments it forms have ministers and deputy ministers from all the component parties. There are other symbols of the unity of the Barisan Nasional such as the BN song and BN manifestos. Although the original coalition is between race-based parties as are some who joined later, a number are non-racial constitutionally.

Chedet.cc blog, 2013

ॐ

At one time the BN had 14 parties representing every race and tribe in Malaysia. Obviously it was difficult to get every party to accept all the policies or objectives of the coalition all the time. PAS and Parti Bersatu Sabah (PBS) left because of disagreement with the decisions made by the centre. Still a majority of the parties stayed with the coalition, and continued cooperating in the governments and during elections. The basis of this cooperation is the principle of sharing; of give and take and of a willingness to sacrifice and concede so as to stay together. This willingness to sacrifice and to share is what makes the BN unique. In the BN no party is able to get all that it considers its entitlement. Consequently no party is absolutely happy with the BN. This is good because all have to make some sacrifice. If any party in the coalition is absolutely happy then one can be sure that something is wrong, that that party has not made the required sacrifice.

Chedet.cc blog, 2013

The Barisan National exemplifies this *kongsi* [or sharing] spirit. To break this kongsi the DAP must antagonise the Chinese against the Malays. Through all the elections in Malaysia, the people of Johore have personified the kongsi principle. In every election the Malays would support the MCA Chinese and the Chinese would support the UMNO Malay candidates resulting in Johore delivering 100 percent BN victories. Now Kit Siang[2] has decided it is time to break up the kongsi. True the Chinese majority in Gelang Patah is smaller than the other constituencies Kit Siang had contested. But Kit Siang hopes with the support of PAS he can split Malay votes, so as to defeat BN. Now UMNO is contesting Gelang Patah with little hope of getting Chinese support. Kit Siang does not agree with the Islamic state and Islamic laws proposed by PAS but that party's ability to break Malay unity in Johore would benefit DAP. Kit Siang knows that PAS would never be strong enough to impose its version of the Islamic laws in Malaysia if Pakatan wins. Kit Siang is more wily than any of PAS's leaders. He also knows that PAS needs the support of the Chinese in order to defeat UMNO. He holds the trump card in any *pakatan*[3] of the opposition. Johore is a Barisan National bastion. If it is broken then he could put an end to the MCA's cooperation with UMNO under the old 'kongsi' or sharing concept. Instead there would be meritocracy in everything where the winner takes all and the devil takes the hindmost.   *Chedet.cc blog,* 2013

ॐ

In the 2008 elections, it was manifestly clear that the BN had lost popularity instead. It scored less than two-thirds for the first time since 1969, gaining only 140 of the 222 seats. The pro-sharing Malays were dismayed but despite changing their leader, they found that the trend towards liberalisation remained. The belief of the new leadership was that Chinese support would come back if the sharing policies of the NEP were not implemented. Despite obviously rejecting the sharing principle, support for the BN did not return. Instead the DAP dangled before the Chinese the possibility of having both political and economic dominance. This was deemed possible because the Malays had split into three parties and each one of them needed Chinese support in order to win. The Chinese had the deciding vote and were in a position to give victory only to those who believe in throwing out the sharing concept.   *Chedet.cc blog,* 2014

ON UMNO

UMNO came into being because of the Malay fear of losing out to the Chinese. The honeymoon period immediately before and after Independence lessened this fear, but it was never really absent. For, so long as the Chinese, or at least the fairly numerous adherents of the Malaysian Chinese Association, cooperated, this fear remained subdued. But the gradual divergence of the leaders from the stated policies of UMNO, and the continuous and more forthright demands of the Chinese within and outside the MCA, soon awakened the old fears. UMNO leaders chose to appease the Chinese, depending partly on the power of patronage and the usual docility of the Malays to keep party followers in line. But the decision to disregard the mild criticisms, and the failure to appreciate the steady defection of supporters soon had its effect. UMNO weakened, until by the time of the 1969 elections, its strength had so eroded that it had to rely on promises of huge discriminatory government spending in order to gain support in some stubborn areas.

The Malay Dilemma, 1970

&

We do not want power for its own sake but only as a means for maintaining our position.

Selangor UMNO Convention, Selayang, 1982

&

In UMNO lies the aspirations of the Malays. All that we have today is because of UMNO's struggles. We shoved aside the Malayan Union, we achieved Independence, we filled this independence with development, we improved our economy and Malays' education through the strength we gained from UMNO.

UMNO General Assembly, Kuala Lumpur, 1987

There were tragedies and bad incidents in post-Independence Malaysia. But the UMNO-led government survived all these crises. All crises were temporary because of the efficiency of the UMNO leadership. As long as UMNO remains strong, it will continue to overcome its problems.

UMNO General Assembly, Kuala Lumpur, 1987

ॐ

The problem of UMNO leaders today is that while they aspire to embrace the mountain, but alas, their hands cannot reach. Like a short blanket, it covers the chest but the thighs are exposed, it covers the thighs but the chest is left bare. Whatever we do, we will hurt our closest ones. This is the problem which afflicts anyone who leads UMNO.

UMNO General Assembly, Kuala Lumpur, 1987

ॐ

We know that history holds in high esteem UMNO's achievement all these years. It is now up to us to ensure what history will say of us today and in years to come. Remember, none among us, including myself, are important. There is not one UMNO member or leader who is important, whatever their post. This organisation, UMNO, is important as a body which will change the lives of Malays. Without UMNO, there is nothing anyone of us can do no matter how clever or smart we are.   *UMNO General Assembly, Kuala Lumpur, 1987*

ॐ

Many Malays believe that there is really no difference between PAS and UMNO. Many declare that whereas UMNO has no choice but to depend on the Malays, the Malays are not so constrained. They have a choice between UMNO and PAS. If they choose PAS, nothing bad would really happen to them. In fact PAS is likely to be more Islamic and this would fit well with the religious aspirations of the Malay Muslims.

Malaysia in the New Millennium conference, London, 2000

So far PAS has ruled Kelantan and Terengganu. Is there anything wrong with these states which indicate that the party will mess up the whole country? PAS claims, and many Malays believe, that anything that UMNO has done for the Malays and the country any government could do. PAS as the central government of Malaysia would be able to protect Malay special privileges and carry out the same affirmative action by giving the Malays special preference for scholarships, business licences and opportunities, preserve Malay reserves, etc. It is possible that PAS can do all these but special privileges are of little use if you have no idea how to make use of them. UMNO had devised many strategies to take advantage of the special privileges in order to enhance the position of the Malays.   *Malaysia in the New Millennium Conference, London,* 2000

ॐ

We need to look after our children, to ensure they do not hate UMNO. If we are disunited, it will be easy for outsiders to bring us under their control.

Kepala Batas, Penang, 2000

ॐ

I quit UMNO in May of 2008. I had been a member for almost 60 years but I no longer recognised the party as the one I had served for most of my life.

A Doctor in the House, 2011

ON LAW AND ORDER

I may add, at this point, that the independence of the judiciary also implies the independence of the legislature from the judiciary. This is a topical and relevant comment because there is a tendency for institutions wishing to be autonomous to believe that while others should not interfere in their affairs, they should be free to intrude in the affairs and usurp the functions of others.

Tun Razak Memorial Lecture, Universiti Malaya, Kuala Lumpur, 1977

Research findings, I am told, have also revealed that the dadah[4] problem in a sinister way is very democratic in that it does not discriminate against religion, racial descent, or socioeconomic background of a person. Youths and members of societies from developed as well as developing countries are subjected to serious risk of dadah abuse.

International Conference of NGOs on Dadah Use, Prevention and Control, Kuala Lumpur, 1981

Dadah is one enemy that we cannot say, 'If we cannot fight its abuse, we can join in the abuse.' The obvious answer to the problem is to move on a broad front, i.e. to tackle both the underlying and the related dadah problem together. The government of Malaysia is committed to doing this. And towards the objective of ridding this country of dadah use and substance abuse, the government will not tolerate petty jealousies between groups or professions.

International Conference of NGOs on Dadah Use, Prevention and Control, Kuala Lumpur, 1981

I will always respect the independence of the judiciary. We do not expect the courts to be pro- or anti-government, only pro the Constitution and pro the law [...] We shall always respect their judgments. But the right to make laws must necessarily be that of the legislature.

ASEAN Law Association General Assembly, Universiti Malaya, Kuala Lumpur, 1982

In accordance with our insistence on efficiency, I will see to it that the judiciary will be given what it really needs by way of manpower and physical facilities (though not what it imagines it needs) to enable it to administer justice expeditiously and efficiently. I have been trained to comfort, soothe and to cure – I will always respect the Bar and their independence. I promise that no member of the legal profession would ever be penalised in the course of discharging their duties.

ASEAN Law Association General Assembly, Universiti Malaya, Kuala Lumpur, 1982

A long-winded lawyer was arguing a technical case in a court. He had rambled on in such a desultory and soporific way that it became difficult to follow his line of thought, and the judge had just yawned very suggestively. With just a trace of sarcasm, the tiresome lawyer ventured to observe: 'I sincerely trust that I am not unduly trespassing on the time of this court.' 'My friend,' replied the judge, 'there is a world of difference between trespassing on time and encroaching upon eternity.'

ASEAN Law Association General Assembly, Universiti Malaya, Kuala Lumpur, 1982

I rather envy the ideas which lawyers have as to how the country should be run and the facility and gay abandon with which they express themselves whenever government did something they disagreed with. As an example of how quick they are on the uptake, I would like to relate to you a story about a doctor who had a lawyer as a patient. The doctor after examining the lawyer said, 'I am afraid there is nothing I can do for you. Your disease is hereditary.' 'Well, in that case,' said the lawyer, 'send the bill to my father.' I also envy the precision with which lawyers use language. For example, in another case, a doctor was treating a lawyer suffering from diabetes and high blood pressure. The doctor advised slimming. He said, 'You are overweight. You weigh nearly 250 pounds. Tell me, what was the least you ever weighed.' The lawyer-patient answered, '8+ pounds'.

ASEAN Law Association General Assembly, Universiti Malaya, Kuala Lumpur, 1982

Malaysia has for some time now addressed itself to the problem of drugs, which has become international in character and knows no national boundaries. It is a creeping menace of alarming proportions that permeates every level of society and threatens to destroy the social fabric of that society. The threat of drugs gives rise not just to problems of a criminal nature, but also has security ramifications that can undermine the survival of a nation. For this reason, Malaysia has legislated harsh laws to curb the drug menace. However, no country can hope to tackle this problem on its own. It requires serious and concerted effort at the international level by all countries and international agencies concerned. Malaysia therefore would like to call on all countries to cooperate in a concerted effort to prevent the production and trafficking of drugs. *Dinner at residence of Swedish Prime Minister Olof Palme, 1985*

On the other hand, we have some obvious though by no means unique flaws. Our 'due process of law' is so slow at times that one might refer to it as the 'overdue process of law'. Justice delayed is justice denied and justice overly delayed is injustice perpetrated. It is no excuse to say that the law's delay is a universal phenomenon. We should seek to do better. The delay cannot be attributed exclusively to the Bench. The blame has to be shared by both sides. Dilatoriness is a crime. Deliberate frustration of the law by whatever means can only lead to injustice in the long run.

Malaysian Law Conference, Kuala Lumpur, 1985

Every legal system can work effectively and efficiently only if all the players play according to both the written and the unspoken rules of the game. Cooperation, not collusion of course, amongst all the practitioners of our system of justice, certainly between those in the legal and judicial service and the Bar, is of clear importance. It goes without saying that the principal players in the system must respect one another and understand each other's problems. *Malaysian Law Conference, Kuala Lumpur, 1985*

I believe that in any discussion on professionalism mention must be made of the importance of honesty and trustworthiness. At its most innocuous, shortchanging a client, not giving of your best, is a form of dishonesty. It is a moral if not a legal crime. In the practice of law, dishonesty is the more pernicious, the more vicious, because very often lives are involved and futures are at risk. I know that your task is made no easier by the presence of less than honest clients. Many simply want a lawyer to tell him how to do what he wants to do, not someone who can advise on what he can or cannot do. Professionals cannot stand aloof, completely unsullied by the dirt of societal corruption, untouched by the tide of social dishonesty that surrounds them. But they must try. And because of their position and their work in society, I believe that the penalty for less than honest lawyers must be more severe than for their businessman counterpart.

Malaysian Law Conference, Kuala Lumpur, 1985

ॐ

The provision for injunction is right and necessary but like all laws it is not to be abused. To do so would put the law into disrepute and the price to pay for that is horrendous. *Malaysian Law Conference, Kuala Lumpur, 1985*

ॐ

Like the Bar Council, I am disappointed that the Appeal Court has overturned the High Court's decision to stop the Malaysian Anti-Corruption Commission from questioning suspects after working hours. We must respect working hours. Criminals should not commit crimes after working hours. Of course police should not investigate crimes after working hours. Firemen should wait until office opens before putting out fires. The same should apply for weekends and public holidays. No questioning, no investigations and no putting out fires during non-working days. What about politics and politicians? Well no politicking outside office hours also. If we have more holidays then the crime rate would go down as crimes should only be committed during working hours. *Chedet.cc blog, 2009*

Having released people and having detained people under the ISA [Internal Security Act], I think I know something about this act and its application. Firstly one must remember that it is a preventive law, that is it is to be applied before a crime is committed. The law cannot be applied after the crime is committed. For this there are other laws. Secondly, it can be applied only in certain specific cases, as for example when there is a threat to the security of the country. A possible armed uprising or possibility of civil violence would constitute a threat to the security of the country. However, it had been used in the past to incarcerate political opponents, as when Aziz Ishak was detained. At this point visitors to this blog are likely to say I did the same. I admit I did detain people under the ISA in the 1987 Ops Lalang[5]. But it was not because they were members of the opposition. The police had informed me that there was likely to be racial clashes over the issue of Chinese education and the intention of some UMNO members to hold a million-strong demonstration in KL. The people detained were not only members of the opposition but included UMNO members. As soon as the threat passed, the detainees were all released. The issue was not political opposition to the government but the threat to national security. I don't expect this explanation would be accepted by my detractors. But that is normal. Detractors would never admit to being wrong.   *Chedet.cc blog,* 2009

ॐ

If you lead a powerful country you can massacre a few millions and all that happens is a statue, as a war hero, will be put up in your honour. If you lead a poor weak country and you act against violence by the opposition, then you may be accused of oppression and tolerating police brutality.

Chedet.cc blog, 2012

Litigations by politicians may be justified. But politicians must accept that as politicians they would be bad-mouthed by their opponents. It is up to them to counter the allegations made. They should not always be suing in court. For Muslims they should be willing to swear properly that there is no truth to the allegations. Often the litigation is intended to shut the mouths of their opponents. In Malaysia when a case is being heard in a court, it becomes sub-judice and comments outside can constitute 'contempt of court'. By suing, the matter becomes sub-judice and the opponents' mouths would be shut. Through repeated appeals the case can be prolonged and the defendants' mouths would remain shut to the advantage of the litigant for years. For the person sued, much money would have to be spent on lawyers. For years he would be assailed with anxiety that he might be found guilty and if he is unable to pay he may be bankrupted. Yet when the defendant wins, the litigant may need to pay cost only, which the court will fix. Often the amount would be a minute fraction of the amount he is sued for. Because the cost to the litigant is so very little, the tendency is to sue for millions. This is grossly unfair to the defendants. If the law is intended to promote justice then the litigant should also suffer from the same anxieties for the length of time of the hearing and if his allegation is baseless he should pay his victim the same amount he sued for.

Chedet.cc blog, 2012

ON CORRUPTION, CRONYISM AND NEPOTISM

The government has promised an administration that is clean, efficient and trustworthy. This promise is made because a government that is clean, efficient and trustworthy will not only speed up the rate of development but will also enable Malaysians to live a better life as a result of practising these virtues. We do not doubt that a government that is clean, efficent and trustworthy will facilitate and improve the machinery of government, further increase productivity and make this nation stable and strong.

Launch of Leadership by Example Campaign, Kuala Lumpur, 1983

❧

The Western media and their economic and other experts seem to believe that Asian governments must all be corrupt and incompetent. Whatever success that they may achieve in developing and enriching their countries must be due to criminal acts involving corruption, nepotism and crony capitalism. That such practices on the scale implied will certainly prevent economic development from becoming successful is ignored. That in fact the benefits of economic development are clearly enjoyed by the majority of the people of these Asian nations is brushed aside. Consistently and repeatedly any mention of Asian governments must be accompanied by derogatory remarks about their corruption, etc. Clearly the view taken by the Western media is racist. But such is their power that no one dares to state this obvious fact.

Prime Ministerial Lecture of the Harvard Club, Kuala Lumpur, 1998

❧

Corruption and greed must be destroyed and eradicated. Corruption and greeed can destroy our nation. All plans to develop the Malays and other Bumiputeras[6] will fail if corruption and greed become part of our culture. Everything will be ruined if corrupt individuals become the prime minister or members of the Cabinet.   *UMNO General Assembly, Kuala Lumpur, 2000*

We admit that we are not perfect. We have corruption, cronyism, etc. But so have the rich. Despite our alleged corruption, etc., we have developed our countries and given our people a good life. The market forces which want to eliminate corruption, etc., in our countries have had no noticeable success despite the high cost to us. But they have certainly made fortunes by their manipulations of the currencies and the market and now by their acquisition of the banks, industries and businesses.   *South Summit, Havana, Cuba, 2000*

ॐ

We admit that there are abuses in the management of our countries by some of our governments. But our detractors should remember that they had also abused their governments' power when they seized land belonging to the indigenous people and exterminated them, claiming that it was their 'Manifest Destiny', the 'White Man's Burden', to bring civilisation by setting up their own countries in these lands and confining the indigenous people to barren reserves, with no role in the government of the new nations. What they had done to the indigenous people is not out of character for in their own countries they had carried out pogroms against the Jews, inquisitions and mock trials, torture and killing by burning at the stakes.

United Nations General Assembly, New York, 2003

ॐ

Corruption afflicts every country in the world. It is the degree of corruption that determines the success or otherwise of a government's ability to develop the economic potential of a country; where corruption is openly accepted as a way of life, no country can develop and prosper. The business community fears corruption but some welcome it. What is certain is that corruption, by increasing the cost of doing business, will hinder the progress of a country. Although anti-corruption efforts seldom succeed in putting an end to corruption, it is probably successful in slowing down or halting the spread of corruption. That is good enough. Political instability and corruption are the two most important obstructions to business and wealth creation. We of the South must overcome these weaknesses if we want to see business activities prosper our countries.

Non-Aligned Movement Business Forum on South–South Cooperation, Kuala Lumpur, 2003

Let me now turn to a consideration of corruption as an impediment and obstacle to sustainable development. Corruption obviously is a cost, an unnecessary and an unproductive cost. Worse still, it has a way of escalating, and so continuously reducing the competitiveness of a country, something that is terribly important for Malaysia whose trade is twice the size of its GDP. We just cannot afford the additional cost. Unless we fight corruption now, we run the risk of corruption becoming endemic. Illegal gratification is attractive because of the obvious immediate personal gains. It is difficult to convince the corrupt that he will lose even if he is not caught. But in the long run he will have to pay up. A country where corruption is a way of life will never be able to develop, no matter how rich it may be. And a country which remains poor cannot possibly give a good life to the corrupt.

Transparency International Malaysia National Integrity Medal Awards, Kuala Lumpur, 2003

ፈ

There is corruption in the civil service but it is minimal and does not affect the work of government too much. An anti-corruption agency investigates allegations of corruption or when something does not seem right. No one is spared, not even the ministers and prime ministers.

Bangladesh–Malaysia Business Forum, Dhaka, Bangladesh, 2004

ፈ

Corruption is a very major problem in our country. And we should begin to teach that corruption is evil, right from the stage when they are in the kindergarten. Anything that they do that may resemble corruption should be stopped at once. They must be told that this is a sin, and this is bad, this is going to destroy you, it is going to destroy your country. That must be implanted in the child when he is small.

Perdana Discourse Series 3, Perdana Leadership Foundation, Putrajaya, 2005

ፈ

Not too much faith must be placed in anti-corruption laws. When even the law enforcers are corrupt, laws will be ineffective but there must be laws and there must be enforcers. *Asia Human Resource Development Congress, Jakarta, 2006*

The people must be taught from the time they are small to look upon corruption as filthy and criminal. In the homes, in the schools, in the universities and the work places, corruption must be fought with education on the evils of the practice, on how it stifles growth and, in the end, how everyone will have to pay the price.

Asia Human Resource Development Congress, Jakarta, 2006

৯৯

When the New Economic Policy began to show some results in the early 1980s, the Western press and local opponents of the government began to talk about cronyism. Whoever succeeded in a developing country like Malaysia, did so because they were the chosen favourites of the government, particularly the head of the government. I came in for virulent attacks because some Malays actually did well in business. They were all labelled my cronies whether they were indeed my cronies or not. Anyone who succeeded was immediately defined as my crony. Many close friends, relatives and members of my family who failed in business would not be called cronies. It is not the actual relation or association with the leader that qualifies one to be the crony of the prime minister. It is the success of the individual. Failures, no matter how close they may be to the prime minister, would not be called cronies.

Chedet.cc blog, 2008

৯৯

Corruption is a social disease found all over the world. No country is absolutely free from corruption. In some countries corruption has become institutionalised. And corruption is among the most difficult crimes to detect and even more difficult to gain conviction in courts of law.

Global Competitive Forum, Riyadh, Saudi Arabia, 2009

৯৯

Corruption is the single most important obstruction to a country's development. Good decisions cannot be made and even bad decisions would face a lot of delays. In the end most of the investments for the development of the country just would not come in.

Global Competitive Forum, Riyadh, Saudi Arabia, 2009

Corruption is endemic. There is no country in the world that is free of corruption. Even in those countries where the corrupt would be executed, corruption still persists.

Lagos, Nigeria, 2009

≥●

Corruption is a function of the culture of the people, i.e. their value system. When people have no sense of shame and their greed overcomes their better judgement, corruption just cannot be stopped. No amount of explanation about the destructive effect of corruption would be of any use.

Lagos, Nigeria, 2009

≥●

Many ways have been tried to stop corruption. Laws have been passed and the most severe punishment prescribed. Agencies have been set to prevent corruption and to enforce the law. But the result is quite dismal. I will stress once again the need to have an incorruptible leader. Even in a fairly clean society, if the person who gets into power is corrupt, all the cleanliness would disappear very quickly. It is admittedly easier to spread corrupt culture than to erase or reduce it.

Lagos, Nigeria, 2009

≥●

It seems logical and right that those who receive illegal gratification should be considered guilty of breaking the law and should therefore be punished. But, when we talk of corruption, we think of those endowed with power abusing their power in order to gain personal benefit. We think [of] those who offer gratification as being the victim and [that they] should be given some consideration. But the law says that those who pay for the service they receive should also be considered as guilty and should be equally deserving of punishment. Since both the giver and the recipient may be charged with corruption, both would be unwilling to report the incident. This of course makes corruption difficult if not impossible to be brought to a court of law and tried successfully.

Chedet.cc blog, 2009

When winning at all cost becomes obsessive, there will be corruption and abuses of power, more often by the ruling party but also by the opposition. Where people are inclined towards violence, there will be assassinations of candidates and supporters, there will be riots and breakdown of law and order. *International Forum on Pathways of Democratic Transitions, Cairo,* 2011

୨ଈ

Corruption is found everywhere, including in the most developed countries. It cannot be eliminated altogether but it can be reduced. The most important player in the fight against corruption is the executive head of government. If he is incorruptible, he may be able to act against corrupt members of his government and others. If he himself is corrupt, there will be no way for corruption to be curbed. In fact a corrupt head of government will cause corruption to spread throughout the whole administration. With this the country will simply fail.

International Forum on Pathways of Democratic Transitions, Cairo, 2011

ON LEADERSHIP

It is pointless for the leaders to urge others to do good if they themselves do not practise what they preach. It is true that leaders, being human, are not free from errors. However, the public is willing to forgive mistakes if they are made unintentionally and for so long as efforts are made to do good and mistakes are corrected. What I mean by mistake here is not correcting false accusations that are often made but correcting truly genuine mistakes. To spread vicious lies is a heinous act that should not be done by anyone.

Launch of Leadership by Example Campaign, Kuala Lumpur, 1983

To lead by providing good examples is the most effective way to ensure that good deeds are practised by all. There can be no gain by saying one thing but doing another. *Launch of Leadership by Example Campaign, Kuala Lumpur, 1983*

The first good example that we must show is cleanliness in all its aspects, both morally and physically. To be morally clean means to possess good thoughts and ideals and to carry out our duties as promised without any ulterior motive or unworthy intentions. We should not delay our work for the purpose of procuring bribes. What is not rightfully ours should not be taken. We should not be involved in any form of crime or bribery. We should not misuse or abuse authority and we should not be arrogant.

Launch of Leadership by Example Campaign, Kuala Lumpur, 1983

We have heard the saying that nothing is more powerful than an idea whose time has come. I am one who believes that it must be one of the fundamental tasks of true leadership to take a powerful idea and to make its time come. The opportune time, like good luck, may happen by chance. But it more often comes about by the sweat of our brows and by the courage of our convictions, by human effort allied to human determination.

ASEAN Ministerial Meeting, Kuala Lumpur, 1985

Leadership by example means the top men coming to office earlier and wearing nametags instead of privileged disregard of rules by the executives including the prime minister. *World Management Congress, Kuala Lumpur, 1985*

ॐ

The last 1,000 years, or more specifically the last 200 years, have also seen the emergence of exceptional men who tower over their fellow men and have become legends in their own time. We have seen the likes of Mahatma Gandhi, who dared to face the might of the most powerful colonial power with nothing but loin cloth and a mantle of raw courage and conviction around himself. We have seen the likes of Martin Luther King who raised the consciousness of the Afro-American people to recognise that might is not right, and that power can come from a conviction, and from moral righteousness. And finally, we have the likes of Nelson Mandela, who has displayed not to just one country, not just to one race, not to just one continent, but to all of mankind, the highest quality of the humaneness of humanity – a man who stands as a giant among men, as an awe-inspiring example of one who forgave those who had erred, and thus has given a new meaning to the old adage 'To err is human, to forgive divine'.

Africa–Asia Business Forum, Kuala Lumpur, 1999

ॐ

Dato' Seri Abdullah Ahmad Badawi, on the other hand, must be irked by his failure to get a two-thirds majority in Parliament. It is therefore unable to revise the amendments to the Constitution made by previous Barisan Nasional governments or to introduce his own amendments to the Constitution. In any case not getting the usual two-thirds majority is like losing almost. He knows he is regarded as a weak leader of a weak government. His coalition partners do not show much respect for him even though they themselves are weak. And the opposition openly declare they want him to go on leading simply because he is weak; a kind of backhanded compliment. *Chedet.cc blog, 2008*

Today the leader plays a much bigger role. He must therefore be a person of good character who has shown by his previous record to be one who loves his country and his people more than himself. He may have weaknesses but they must be within his control. He needs to be well educated and have sufficient understanding about all fields of human endeavour. And he must have ideas far more than those who serve under him. He has to be the model for the people he leads. He must live the life he advocates for others. He must be prepared to be the first to carry out what he preaches. He has to be brave, disciplined, and capable of fighting his own base inclinations.

Lagos, Nigeria, 2009

ê

There is no shame in quitting but there is a lot of shame in trying to stay on after having failed. This being so, a leader needs to know as much as possible about the problems he is dealing with before deciding. Consultants can help but, in the end, the leader must choose. From then on he must bear the blame if anything goes wrong. Of course he can claim credit if things go right.

Lagos, Nigeria, 2009

ê

Today's leaders are usually elected. This puts an extra burden on him because he must not only rule well but he must carry the people with him. He has to be a juggler, deciding between what he considers is right and what his followers think is right. Sectarianism may compel him to discriminate in favour of the majority group. He would then expose himself not only to accusations of unfairness and bias but he might have to go against his own conscience and better judgement. If he is smart he may be able to do both, retain sectarian support without troubling his own conscience.

Lagos, Nigeria, 2009

ê

The leader or CEO of a state requires almost superhuman skills. But it is only almost superhuman, not really superhuman. So it is still possible not to just survive but to manage things well.   *Lagos, Nigeria, 2009*

ON RACE AND RACE RELATIONS

What went wrong? Obviously a lot went wrong. In the first place, the government started off on the wrong premise. It believed that there had been racial harmony in the past and that the Sino-Malay cooperation to achieve independence was an example of racial harmony. It believed that the Chinese were only interested in business and acquisition of wealth, and that the Malays wished only to become government servants. These ridiculous assumptions led to policies that undermined whatever superficial understanding there was between Malays and non-Malays. On top of this, the government, glorying in its massive strength, became contemptuous of criticisms directed at it either by the opposition or its own supporters. The gulf between the government and the people widened so that the government was no longer able to feel the pulse of the people or interpret it correctly. It was therefore unable to appreciate the radical change in the thinking of the people from the time of Independence and as the 1969 elections approached. And finally when it won by such a reduced majority, the government went into a state of shock which marred its judgement. And so murder and arson and anarchy exploded on May 13, 1969.

That was what went wrong.   *The Malay Dilemma,* 1970

                                    ❧

There never was true racial harmony. There was a lack of interracial strife. There was tolerance. There was accommodation. There was a certain amount of give and take. But there was no harmony. There was in fact cacophony, muted but still audible. And periodically the discordant notes rose and erupted into isolated or widespread racial fights. Racial harmony in Malaysia was therefore neither real nor deep-rooted. What was taken for harmony was absence of open interracial strife. And absence of strife is not necessarily due to lack of desire or reasons for strife. It is more frequently due to a lack of capacity to bring about open conflict.   *The Malay Dilemma,* 1970

We must not forget 1969 because it was a lesson to us of the dangers of racial inequality and race politics.

Anniversary Dinner of Fei San Malaysia, Kuala Lumpur, 1982

ॐ

I feel that before anyone makes an issue out of something there must be a clear understanding of what it is all about. We must realise that in many instances we are faced with the danger of racial conflict that can obstruct our national development.   *Anniversary Dinner of Fei San Malaysia, Kuala Lumpur, 1982*

ॐ

One of the things that the new government did was to lift the ban on my book *The Malay Dilemma*. This is necessary because it is important that the people in this country know what was written in the book rather than hear about it from people whose intentions may not be very healthy. The book will be translated into Chinese, Tamil and Bahasa Malaysia so as to enable everyone to read it if they wish. I am not trying to advertise my book nor am I seeking monetary gain. But I would like to explain that the book was written in 1969–70 and the views reflect the situation prevailing at that time. Today much of the things I describe no longer hold true. After 10 years of the New Economic Policy, a lot of the wrongs have been rectified. The harsh words used in the book may no longer be justified. Indeed the harsh words used in 1969 and 1970 by everyone would seem out of place now.

Anniversary Dinner of Fei San Malaysia, Kuala Lumpur, 1982

ॐ

The Chinese guilds have played a very important part in the social and economic life of Malaysia. Now that we have reached a stage for an economic take-off it is imperative that you organise yourself to play a greater role. The racial exclusiveness of the guilds should be minimised slowly so that everyone in the same field of economic activity would be able to participate. This will not only help strengthen the economy but it will improve the racial harmony in this country. With greater interracial harmony the march to prosperity would be enhanced. I am not forcing this view on you but I do hope you will give it your earnest consideration.

Anniversary Dinner of Fei San Malaysia, Kuala Lumpur, 1982

What Malaysia does in order to solve the problem of ethnic relations is not by any means the ideal. But the exodus that we see in Indochina, for example, has not been seen in Malaysia. The vast majority of non-indigenous Malaysians prefer to stay in Malaysia. Indeed, most of them show by deed and words that they accept the need to identify with the indigenous people and to reduce the chasm between them.

Universiti Malaya, Kuala Lumpur, 1983

৯৬

We have to be conscious as well as concerned with the ethnic dimension of our Malaysian life. To be otherwise is to delude ourselves. It is an accepted fact that homogeneity is becoming less and less the dominant feature of modern states. While we can blame history for it, it is a reality that we have to accept and live with, and more so, it will be the reality for the future because of greater contacts and communication among societies. The multiracial nature of our society is a fact. It is something that every Malaysian must accept, live and cope with.

Universiti Malaya, Kuala Lumpur 1983

৯৬

Malaysia is a multiracial country. Other countries can claim to be multiracial but generally the people of different racial origins are assimilated, speak one national language and have one national culture. To be an American citizen, the immigrant has to speak English and generally absorb local culture.
In Malaysia, the different races do not have to speak the national language and they continue to practise their own cultures. If you can imagine the US with 40 percent Vietnamese, 50 percent Caucasians and 10 percent blacks, all practising their own cultures and speaking their own languages, then you may have some idea of the multiracial character of Malaysia and the problems to be faced when administering it. Many countries in Europe and America are not able to deal with even small doses of inassimilable people.

EMF Foundation Round Table, Kuala Lumpur, 1986

The British were also responsible for the biggest headache that Malaysia faces today – race relations. The British brought in Chinese and Indians without thinking at all about the effect on the Malays. Today we are saddled with the problem of managing three separate races with three separate incompatible cultures and religions. If today these people are not at each others' throats it is certainly not due to any help from others.

Dinner hosted by the British-Malaysian Society, London, 1987

૨▲

In most countries citizenship requires total cultural and linguistic identification with the definitive people of the country. A Chinese Australian or a Chinese American or a Chinese Canadian is more Australian or American or Canadian than a Chinese Malaysian or a Malaysian Chinese is Malaysian. Certainly a Chinese in Thailand, Indonesia or the Philippines is more identified with the indigenous native people there than a Malaysian Chinese is with the Malays and other indigenous people of Malaysia.

International Chinese Newspapers Convention, Kuala Lumpur, 1990

૨▲

That special attention has not been given to Malaysian Indians does not mean that the government does not give attention at all to overcome the problems of the Malaysian Indians.   *MIC General Assembly, Kuala Lumpur, 1996*

૨▲

In a multiracial country like Malaysia, it is difficult to avoid displeasing one race or another at any one time.

Malaysia in the New Millenium Conference, London, 2000

૨▲

Will another May 13 occur when the government becomes weak or a new government is put in place? I am not trying to threaten but the possibility is very real.   *Malaysia in the New Millenium Conference, London, 2000*

Unfortunately, the original practitioners of racial cooperation are now faced with the politics of hatred, religious deviationism, racism and street violence. It is difficult to understand why people in a peaceful rapidly developing Malaysia should want to imitate the ways of countries which have not been able to stay peaceful and to develop. But the fact is that some in Malaysia are not happy that the country is peaceful and the economy is doing well. They hanker after turmoil and violence, injury and death even. They are forever looking for issues and incidents to exploit.

Parliament House, Kuala Lumpur, 2001

૨▲

Malaysia is a multiethnic country. The majority is made up of the indigenous Malays and other tribal people. Then there are big Indian and Chinese minorities. The races are divided further because ethnicity is linked with religious differences, cultural and linguistic differences and, most important of all, the disparities in terms of wealth. Ethnic difference is usually enough to create tension in the relations between races. But with all the other differences and in particular the disparities in wealth, tension and confrontation between the races would seem inevitable. The philosophy is very simple. If one race grabs all political or economic power for itself there would be strong antagonism from the other races, there would be political instability and there would be violent confrontations. No economic growth or development could take place. In that situation the race which takes all for itself will find that it would be owning all of nothing, all of a country that is politically unstable, perhaps involved in civil war and with an economy that not only fails to grow but could actually be shrinking. So in the end the race which grabs everything will find that it has nothing.

CIMA Global Leaders Summit, Colombo, Sri Lanka 2005

૨▲

Difficulties in assimilation arise when the latecomers are more dynamic and better equipped to progress than the indigenous people. A feeling of superiority towards the indigenous people tended to keep the latecomers apart. As their community grew, they established separate enclaves and erected invisible barriers against the indigenous. As their numbers grew, the separation became deeper. *Chedet.cc blog, 2008*

The non-Malays in Malaysia have a lot of sensitive issues too. We cannot touch on them. We would be accused of being racist, being insensitive, provocative and offensive. But supposing we ignore their sensitivities and we talk loudly about them. They would not like it. They may reply in kind, perhaps more insultingly. Then we have to increase our insulting remarks in order to annoy, knowing that what we say would irritate and anger them. The end result must be tension between the races in Malaysia which may lead to violence, continuous violence. Lives may be lost and property destroyed. You can tell relatives of the people killed or owners of the property destroyed that this is okay, this is human rights, this is freedom, this is democracy. Think they will celebrate and offer more of their relatives to be killed so that you can behave insensitively?

Chedet.cc blog, 2008

꿍

What we are witnessing today is an explosion of racial politics that is more bitter and blatant than ever before. Even the least observant cannot fail to notice how Malaysian politics now is more about racial inequities than about liberalism, human rights, openness, etc. True there has been quite a lot of discussion on the ISA. But most of the angry and bitter discussion is about Malay 'privileges', about the Social Contract, about the deputy prime minister and prime minister being Malays, about UMNO bullying, about being or not being immigrants, about Malay dominance. Even the criticisms regarding the way judges are appointed or promoted have elements of race that is hardly disguised. Truly Malaysian politics has not been decoupled from racial sentiments and loyalties. And it is going to remain so for as long as the different races prefer to be separated and divided, prefer to strongly uphold their languages, cultures and their historical origins and links.

Chedet.cc blog, 2008

We take the relative peace and stability in our country for granted. But look at other multiethnic countries. In most cases the indigenous people, if given power would not just discriminate against what they consider to be non-indigenous people but would want to expel them. Look around us and you will understand what I mean. Look at the Tamils of Sri Lanka, and the Indians in Burma. There are other examples which I will not mention here. But the indigenous people of this country actually welcome the non-indigenous and expressed their willingness to share the wealth and the opportunities that this great country has to offer between them. But the sharing must be fair. That was the kind of sharing our founders agreed upon.   *Chedet.cc blog,* 2008

ॐ

In Malaysia we are constantly being asked to confront each other on racial issues. Disputes cannot be resolved by rigidity in our stand. But we have to be rigid if we do not want to be vilified. It is a miracle that this multiracial country has remained stable and peaceful for so long. If the extremists can have their way we would all be at each others' throats. We would be demonstrating in the streets and at the airports. If we do not accede to the wishes of the extremists then we cannot even make a living, there will be no investments and no jobs for the workers. Today we are grappling with the problem of education. We have three streams and woe betide anyone who suggests that we should not have them. We talk of liberal society, of free speech, but if you express some commonsensical views you would be labelled racist.   *Chedet.cc blog,* 2009

ॐ

In Malaysia today the label that has effectively prevented the truth from being heard is 'racism' and 'racist'. Fear of these labels has prevented the truth from countering the lies that have been spun and spread. There is no doubt that such a thing as racism exists. It is the extremism which reflects the mindless and belligerent championing of race regardless of the rights and wrongs involved. But to argue in favour of one's race based entirely on truth and proven facts, to argue in order to correct wrong assumptions and deliberate lies, to defend the truth and to expose lies – these are not manifestations of racism, nor is the speaker a racist.   *Chedet.cc blog,* 2010

It is clear that in Malaysia, even though multiracial parties cannot truly be formed, but multiracial cooperation through a coalition of race-based parties is possible, viable and sustainable. In fact the opposition finally decided to copy the BN formula. However, the cooperation among the opposition partners does not amount to a true coalition. It is only meant to avoid their parties from contesting against each other during elections. The parties retain their identities and their symbols. There is no common platform or objectives. The cooperation is friable and, indeed, in the present elections they are not able to avoid contesting against each other. Should the opposition Pakatan win, the government they form would not be stable and would be incapable of deciding on the numerous unpopular policies and laws that a government is expected to adopt or enact.   *Chedet.cc blog,* 2013

❧

Malaysians, be they Malays, Chinese, Indians or the natives of Sabah and Sarawak must banish from their minds the idea of racial dominance. This country must be shared and shared fair by all the races.

                                                             Chedet.cc blog, 2014

ON UNITY

The natural tendency is for disintegration rather than integration. Hence, the
need for a conscious effort at integration.

Universiti Malaya, Kuala Lumpur, 1983

ॐ

Politicians see in racial chauvinism an issue demanding to be exploited.
Journalists see too good a story to be bypassed merely for the sake of
national unity.

Universiti Malaya, Kuala Lumpur, 1983

ॐ

It is obvious that we are not going to achieve full unity, nor can we remove
ethnic conflict completely. Any course that we set for ourselves will result
in unhappiness for someone or others. If we are to favour one particular
ethnic group, we will make them happy but the rest very unhappy indeed.
If we favour anyone of the other groups, we are going to get the same result.
So, since we cannot make everyone happy and satisfied, nor can we favour
just one of the groups, the only choice left to us is to make everyone equally
unhappy. Thus no one group is favoured in Malaysia. Even the indigenous
people are not getting all that they ask for, and are consequently just as
unhappy and dissatisfied as are the non-indigenous.

Universiti Malaya, Kuala Lumpur, 1983

ॐ

Even in countries populated by people of only one race, the animosity
between rich and poor, urban and rural can reach the stage when rebellions
break out. If the rich and poor, urban and rural divisions are amplified by
racial or ethnic divisions as well, the potential for a conflagration is infinitely
greater. Indeed one of the major causes of the 1969 race riots in Malaysia
was due to this division. The formulation of the NEP was therefore an
essential part of the strategy for national integration.

Universiti Malaya, Kuala Lumpur, 1983

If the new generation no longer respects the old generation, then disunity
has occurred in our country.   *Kuala Lumpur, 1986*

॰॰

Malaysia belongs to all of us and is our joint responsibility, but if each
section thinks only of its own rights, the independence of the country
will eventually be lost.   *Kuala Lumpur, 1986*

॰॰

After-dinner speeches are supposed to be light and not too taxing on the
mind. Perhaps this is because after a heavy dinner and possible indigestion
we should be spared mental indigestion as well. National unity is not a
suitable post-prandial subject. But then it is your president [Tan Sri Ahmad
Sarji, President of the Harvard Club of Malaysia] who chose this subject.
I have no say in the matter. If you get indigestion both gastronomically
and cerebrally, you should know whom to blame.

Speech on a United Malaysian Nation by Year 2020, Kuala Lumpur, 1992

॰॰

Some nations evolve naturally through ethnicity and a common culture.
Others, and this includes Malaysia, are legally constituted nations. There is
no common inherited ethnicity or culture. There is no naturally common
language. Even the geographical boundaries did not evolve. They are
delineated by common consent through a process of negotiations. In the
Peninsula the common factor is provided by the recognition of the federation
of the Malay States as the basis for the nation. But by the time of Independence
these states had already been changed through linkages instituted by the
British. Additionally the population had changed so that a common ethnic
origin cannot be the basis of national unity. The presence of citizens of
differing ethnic and cultural origins requires the formulation of a new basis
for national unity. Fortunately for Malaysia the founding fathers were able to
reach broad agreement on the basis for this unity. This sociopolitical contract
bound together the citizens of Malaya and, with minor modifications, has been
accepted by the peoples of Sabah and Sarawak when Malaysia was formed.

Speech on a United Malaysian Nation by Year 2020, Kuala Lumpur, 1992

National unity in our multiethnic and multireligious country can only
be maintained and strengthened if there is a high level of understanding,
tolerance and mutual respect amongst our diverse peoples.

Last Speech as Prime Minister in the Dewan Rakyat, Kuala Lumpur, 2003

৯৯

We have to constantly and tirelessly work to strengthen national unity and
take immediate action to curb tendencies that could work against the national
interest. No one should have a narrow viewpoint and accuse the government
of trying to destroy the culture and language of any race. In reality it is only
in Malaysia that the interests of all races are safeguarded and financed by the
government.   *Last Speech as Prime Minister in the Dewan Rakyat, Kuala Lumpur, 2003*

৯৯

Malaysia has a multiracial population but is quite unique in that the division
is not just by race alone but by religion, language, culture and economic
situation. Unity in such a diversity is extremely difficult to achieve. If we
study other nations where people of different ethnic groups have immigrated,
we will find that integration and unity depended on several important factors.
Firstly the indigenous people or the people who had set up the country make
up, at least initially, a very big proportion of the population. Additionally
they would be dominant and materially successful. The small numbers of
immigrants trickling in found it judicious and beneficial to be identified
with the numerically superior and powerful dominant inhabitants. They
would willingly forget their original languages and adopt the language of
the people of the country as well as their culture; they would intermarry
and over time they would be totally absorbed and assimilated and identified
with the indigenous people. In such a situation unity is not a problem.
The United States is one such country where the original language and
basic culture of first settlers are accepted by later immigrants. In the old
days, before the coming of the Europeans, the few Chinese and Indians
who settled in Malacca adopted the language and much of the culture of
the Malays [...] Unfortunately when later the China-born Chinese-
speaking immigrants dominated in numbers as well as economic wealth,
the Malay-speaking Baba and Nyonya [...] reverted to being Chinese in
every way possible.   *Chedet.cc blog, 2008*

The leaders of the different races were, at least in the beginning, able to get along well with each other. They developed close friendships. But they had to be very conscious of their racial backing and to cater to racial demands. The lower ranking leaders, the ordinary members of political parties and the people as a whole had shown no sign of forgetting their racial identity. There may be few liberal-minded ones who reject race, but some who do this do so because they believe their own race would gain by it. So even these people are racialist at heart. Then came the resurgence of Islam worldwide. The Malaysian Malays began to adopt Islamic conservativeness, especially with the dress code. This tended to push them further apart from the non-Muslims who saw this as an attempt to differentiate Muslim Malaysians from non-Muslim Malaysians. Some people suspect that this is the intention. The behaviour of some extremist exponents of Islamic separateness did not help. And so the races drifted further and further apart. All the time the so-called non-racial parties with their single-minded campaign against the positions of the Malays and Islam as agreed upon at the beginning actually intensified Malay racial sentiments, causing them to yearn for Malay unity rather than Malaysian unity. The ideal of having a non-racial Malaysian nationality has now been almost forgotten. *Chedet.cc blog,* 2008

ON RELIGION

Whereas animism was the indigenous religion of the Malays, Hinduism and Islam were foreign in origin. These religions came with the Indian and Arab traders who not only traded, but also settled in the towns and married into the well-established Malay families in these towns. In time, these mixed families became rich and very influential. The social and economic differences between the town and the country became more marked. The townsfolk set a pace which the country folk found increasingly difficult to emulate.

The Malay Dilemma, 1970

❧

As far as Islamic family law is concerned in this country, it applies only to Muslims. It is not the law for the whole country. If a person is not a Muslim, he will not be affected.

Meeting of Multi-Faith Consultative Council, Kuala Lumpur, 1990

❧

Islam is the most misunderstood religion today. It is misunderstood not only by non-Muslims but by Muslims themselves. Such is the misunderstanding of Muslims about their religion that they have erected a tall barrier against access to it and to the Muslims themselves by non-Muslims. They seem to have forgotten that most Muslims had ancestors who were not Muslims but who were converted to Islam because they came into contact with Muslims. Had the Muslims of the past rejected contact with non-Muslims, then the ancestors of the present-day Muslim would not have learnt about Islam and would not have converted to Islam. If they had not, then the present-day Muslim might have been born non-Muslim and would not be Muslim.

International Conference of Religious Studies, Kuala Lumpur, 1999

Despite the repeated injunction that Muslims must seek well-being in this life as much as in the hereafter, many Muslims believe that a Muslim should only seek merit for the next world. Consequently he neglects his well-being in this world and this results in Muslims becoming poor and unable to help themselves and to prevent themselves from being oppressed by others.

International Conference of Religious Studies, Kuala Lumpur, 1999

The Muslim's failure to understand his own religion is nothing compared to the failure of the non-Muslims, in particular the ethnic Europeans, to understand the Muslims and their religion. There is a historical basis for this. The long period of Muslim dominance and occupation of substantial parts of Europe has permanently affected the European psyche. The Crusade against the Muslims, the struggle to liberate Europe and the Holy Land from the Muslims, seems unending.

International Conference of Religious Studies, Kuala Lumpur, 1999

Although Malaysia is governed by predominantly Malay Muslim governments there has been no attempt to oppress the non-Muslims. The government of Malaysia is very tolerant and shows respect for the religious observances of the different religious groups. No one can say that by being so it is not Islamic.

International Conference of Religious Studies, Kuala Lumpur, 1999

Religion is still very relevant in the Malaysian multi-religious society. To ignore it or to side-line it would be unwise. A totally secular society cannot be created in Malaysia. The religions of the people must play their role.

International Conference of Religious Studies, Kuala Lumpur, 1999

In Malaysia where Islam is the religion of only 60 percent of the people, not only is freedom to practise other religions very meaningful and important but it implies an acceptance of tolerance and accommodation on the part of the majority Muslims. *International Conference of Religious Studies, Kuala Lumpur, 1999*

I believe that religions will still have a role in the 21st century. We are seeing now a swing towards total materialism in the West, where wealth alone is expected to bring about happiness and a better quality of life. But we have only recently experienced how the quest for unlimited wealth by the avaricious can destroy the tranquility of life in our country. Without a religious anchor we would have despaired. But we did not because we could fall back upon our spiritual values. Calmed by our spiritual beliefs, we were able to face the material problems of our life, to understand them and to overcome them. Without spiritual beliefs it is doubtful that we can overcome the challenges without becoming unbalanced.

International Conference of Religious Studies, Kuala Lumpur, 1999

❧

Religion, according to Karl Marx, is the opium of life. But religions have survived and will continue to survive long after Marx and his ideology is relegated to the history books. Clearly ideologies invented by man cannot replace religions. *International Conference of Religious Studies, Kuala Lumpur, 1999*

❧

Religion should be viewed as a way of life, envisioning as its ultimate goal the day when all men can live together in perfect understanding and peace.

General Assembly of the World Evangelical Fellowship, Kuala Lumpur, 2001

❧

Once started, religious strife has a tendency to go on and on, to become permanent feuds. Perhaps religion and deep faith make it impossible for enmity between people of different religious faiths to become reconciled. It is because of this that some advocate abandoning religions and faith in God. Many now openly question the existence or relevance of God.

General Assembly of the World Evangelical Fellowship, Kuala Lumpur, 2001

In multiracial, multicultural Malaysia it is also worthwhile for religious leaders to revisit their roles as we move into a new era in the development of society. The greatest contribution they can make is in promoting tolerance among their followers.

General Assembly of the World Evangelical Fellowship, Kuala Lumpur, 2001

It would seem that despite the peace preached by all the religions of the world, humanity has not mastered the skills and the capacity to live at peace with each other. When it suits us, we are ready to forget religious injunctions or at times to reinterpret religion in order to justify wars. Yet we hear today more talk and exhortation for people, governments especially, to respect human rights and uphold them, to allow for the freedom of choice in the election of governments, for free speech and press freedom. One would think that humanity has become truly civilised even if they are less keen on religious and spiritual values. Some even believe that they can be human and humane without need for religion. They know what values are good and honourable without having to be told by religion about this.

World Fellowship of Buddhists Conference, Shah Alam, 2002

Every time science explains anything about the materials or the phenomena on earth or in the universe, it fails to explain why. Finally science concludes that it is nature. But why should nature determine all these phenomena; from the electron, protons and neutrons, the electrical charges to the stars which are thousands of times bigger than the sun of ours, emitting enormous heat, science cannot explain beyond lamely saying that it is natural.

World Fellowship of Buddhists Conference, Shah Alam, 2002

The ancient religions place more emphasis on spiritual values. Indeed while they do not decry wealth, they do not regard wealth as the deity. Spiritual well-being, peace with oneself and with the world is what the old religions promote.

World Fellowship of Buddhists Conference, Shah Alam, 2002

Sensitivities of people differ. We don't wear chador[7] in Malaysia but go to the countries where the chador is *de rigueur* and wear a miniskirt because it is your right. Then you will see what will happen. Even Queen Elizabeth covered up sufficiently when visiting Saudi Arabia. She was sensitive, her royal rights notwithstanding. *Chedet.cc blog,* 2008

༄

If we care to read the history of the Muslims and the Europeans, we would notice that from around the 15th century of the Christian era when the Muslims rejected what they regarded as non-religious knowledge, the Muslim civilisation began to regress. The Europeans, after acquiring the knowledge of the Muslims, started to emerge from the Dark Ages and to build the civilisation that we see today. Unfortunately Muslim historians seem not to have noticed the significance of the fatwas of the 15th century AD. Even today Muslims seem unwilling to connect this decline of their civilisation with the neglect of non-religious knowledge. But European historians admit that their emergence from the Dark Ages, their Renaissance, coincided with their study of the Islamic civilisation and its origins. *Chedet.cc blog,* 2010

༄

The Muslims worldwide are weak. Naturally they have not raised meaningful objection against the atrocities. It is as if Muslims care only for themselves and not their brothers, yet Islam enjoined upon them the brotherhood of all Muslims. Since the Muslims care not for each other or for Islam, anybody can beat any Muslim to death in full view of the other Muslims. I feel sorry for the Rohingyas. It is their turn today. *Chedet.cc blog,* 2013

ON EDUCATION

Malaysia is a developing country that has implicit faith in education as a means of achieving development goals. This faith is reflected in its budget of which 24 percent is allocated to education.

National Institute of Public Administration, Kuala Lumpur, 1975

At this stage in the development, Malaysia cannot afford disruptions in the educational programmes. The developed countries can have fun and games at their universities but here we are very much inclined towards insisting that universities play their traditional roles, i.e. they should teach and they should do research.

National Institute of Public Administration, Kuala Lumpur, 1975

The universities of today cannot help but be closely identified with the community and the nation. Consequently, students and faculty tend to become embroiled in matters other than learning or teaching or research. By and large this is a good thing. Indeed the Malaysian government has stated again and again that universities should not be ivory towers. But a line has to be drawn between what is healthy and what is sick. Interests which do not obstruct the primary functions of the universities are laudable but acts which obstruct or distract bona fide students and academics from pursuing their primary objectives do not only infringe on personal liberties but hurt the development of the nation. This we cannot afford, at least not at this stage in our development. We are therefore still of the view that universities should concentrate primarily on teaching and doing research. All else must be regarded as secondary and incidental. And certainly all disruptive activities must be regarded as abhorrent, undesirable and unworthy of being permitted to take place.

National Institute of Public Administration, Kuala Lumpur, 1975

I would like to stress here very categorically that the government has no intention whatsoever of changing the character of Chinese primary schools. The provisions in the Constitution that safeguard the rights of using the mother tongue of the various communities in this country will be respected.

Anniversary Dinner of Fei San Malaysia, Kuala Lumpur, 1982

❧

Education is important. Every year thousands graduate from universities and colleges in our country as well as from colleges and universities overseas, and many are being trained in science and technological fields. We are aware that the development of our human resources is equally as important as the development of natural resources. Without indigenous science and technology, the resources of a nation cannot be fully exploited for our development.

Universiti Pertanian Malaysia, Serdang, Selangor, 1983

❧

We are moulding a national education system. To establish a national system, we must have the agreement of all quarters and not of only one side.

Opening of a Chinese-Medium School, Klang, 1990

❧

Students in national schools should be close with students in Chinese and Tamil schools, otherwise they will always harbour suspicions of one another.

Opening of a Chinese-Medium School, Klang, 1990

❧

When we make the massive investments which we must make at the tertiary level, we cannot afford to neglect [...] the primary level where the foundation for learning is laid and where there is a much much bigger bang for the buck.

Second World Knowledge Conference, Kuala Lumpur, 2000

❧

Both the public and private institutions of higher learning will be required to increase the number of Bumiputera graduates and ensure that the courses offered meet market demand.

Parliament House, Kuala Lumpur, 2001

In the past, we changed the English schools, which were open to all races, to national schools to hasten the development of Bahasa Malaysia but the problem is that some people want to mix language with religion and want schools which are more Islamic although religion is taught as a subject.

Universiti Teknologi Petronas, Tronoh, Perak, 2005

إله

In this country, everyone wants to study medicine. Or rather, every Indian wants to study medicine. They think that they would be eligible, and they will get good dowry if they are doctors. Because people with eligible daughters have to pay a very high dowry.

Perdana Discourse Series 3, Perdana Leadership Foundation, Putrajaya, 2005

إله

When you are studying something, please remember that you are actually studying for your children. And if you think that you are doing this thing for your children – not for yourself alone – but for your children, I'm quite sure you will study harder. Unless of course you don't love children. I love children. Never have enough of them.

Perdana Discourse Series 3, Perdana Leadership Foundation, Putrajaya, 2005

إله

It would be a tragedy if we all wanted to study only one subject. Suppose all of us want to study law, imagine what kind of world it would be if all the people in this room were lawyers. It would be a great disaster. You know lawyers can argue both sides. You just assign them. He can defend the crook, he can also become the prosecutor. [The] next day he may become the prosecutor, and he will try and put the crook into jail. My apologies to those people who are trained as lawyers; Shakespeare said 'First thing we do, we hang the lawyers.'

Perdana Discourse Series 3, Perdana Leadership Foundation, Putrajaya, 2005

Schooling and acquisition of knowledge I think can contribute towards creating a Bangsa Malaysia. I must admit that the concept of Sekolah Wawasan[8] did not receive good support, especially from Chinese educationists (these people do not want to have anything to do with the Malays). I feel very sad. We live in the same country, work and play together. So what is wrong with our children meeting in schools? I went to an English school during my time and my classmates were Malays, Chinese and Indians, and I got along fine with them. *Perdana Discourse Series 8, Perdana Leadership Foundation, Putrajaya, 2008*

ॐ

One of my experiences that I went through before I became a minister was when I was still a chairman of the Higher Education Council. There was a day that we had a meeting when I was warned that there would be a demonstration and they wanted to shift the meeting to some other place. I disagreed and continued the meeting and when it ended, I was arrested by students and was put on a kangaroo court trial where they asked many questions which I answered until they didn't know what more to ask. Finally, they complained about the bad condition of the canteen furniture in ITM (UiTM). So I said, ok let's go and see, and I agreed with them that the furniture was really old and needed to be replaced.

Perdana Discourse Series 10, Perdana Leadership Foundation, Putrajaya, 2009

ॐ

I was very impatient when I was the minister of education. Some people led by one person whom I shall not name got the university students to demonstrate. It seemed that somebody in Baling died of starvation. So they demonstrated against the government for allowing a man or boy to die of starvation. But that was an immature kind of thing; when you demonstrate, you cannot do very much. On the other hand, when you are demonstrating, I doubt that you are studying. I did not see them carrying out their books and pens while they were demonstrating. Yes, they used their hands a lot but nothing more beyond that. So they were wasting time, not studying and spent their time demonstrating. This is especially bad when you find that these students had been given an opportunity to acquire university education through other people's money, from the government.

Perdana Discourse Series 10, Perdana Leadership Foundation, Putrajaya, 2009

Based on my observation, when you are studying you must study and study very hard. Even if you have a brilliant brain, if it is not used, it's worthless. In order to acquire knowledge, you have to learn and study. Knowledge doesn't come to you just like that even if you are brilliant.

Perdana Discourse Series 10, Perdana Leadership Foundation, Putrajaya, 2009

૨ટે

When I went to Singapore to study medicine, I found that the number of students there was very small, just 77. Out of 77, seven were Malays, one girl and six boys, one-tenth of the student population. Obviously we need to create more opportunities for other youths to get their education. Malaysia is one of the countries that spends almost a quarter of the allocation of funds for development on education. The first thing we did was to set up a university, and then set up the second and third universities and, lastly, we set up colleges.

Perdana Discourse Series 10, Perdana Leadership Foundation, Putrajaya, 2009

૨ટે

The government has decided that the teaching of science and mathematics would revert to Malay in the government schools, with Chinese in Chinese schools and Tamil in Tamil schools. How this is going to help integrate Malaysians, I do not know. Since then I had conducted a poll on my blog. The result is 84 percent want to retain English as the language medium for these subjects. Admittedly the poll was conducted in the English language and English language speakers might be biased in favour of English. But some parents and teachers had also conducted a survey and the majority are again in favour of English. A petition to the prime minister by parents and teachers was copied to me and they were in favour of retaining English. At least one senior non-Malay politician had left a Barisan Nasional component party and joined the opposition because of the switch back to Malay, Tamil and Chinese. He claimed that he could not afford to send his grandchildren abroad as some who advocate Malay as the medium had been doing.   *Chedet.cc blog,* 2009

History is not a compulsory subject in our schools. If at all history is taught, it is sketchy, not really giving a clear picture of what it was like to be ruled by foreigners, by the British, the Japanese and, in some cases, the Thais. I am not trying to say that those who lived under colonial rule are more appreciative of independence, although that is basically true. But what we should all be concerned with is that we appreciate our independence and our freedom more, whatever may be our political leanings. Is it wrong for us to look back on the past? Some think it is irrelevant. That was before, this is now. Don't tell us all those stories about the struggles of people gone by. We have always been independent. All our life we have been independent. But I think we should know where we came from. Otherwise we would not know which way we should go. We may think we are going forward when in fact we are going backwards, back to where we started. We would not be making progress. I am pleading for the teaching of history.   *Chedet.cc blog,* 2009

I'm a stout Malay nationalist but even I cannot keep defending the empty places for Malay students and denying the non-Malays a place in university while the Malay students are still playing.

Perdana Discourse Series 10, Perdana Leadership Foundation, Putrajaya, 2009

ON MALAYS

The Indians and the Arabs changed the pattern of trade in the old Malay sultanates. They not only traded, but some of them settled and married Malays close to the courts of the rajas. Because these merchants had to be astute in business and reasonably rich in order to trade so far from their homeland, it is not surprising that their abilities were soon recognised and utilised by the Malay rajas. They became very influential in the Malay courts and were in time accepted as Malays.   *The Malay Dilemma*, 1970

ॐ

The Malays who achieved Merdeka[9] were not by character quite the same Malays who had allowed the British to overrun their country and displace them with Chinese and Indians. Circumstances leading to Merdeka had forced a different outlook on life in general, a different attitude to surroundings and a different way of approaching and tackling the problems that faced the Malays. For a time it seemed as if they would really break away from their lethargic, self effacing past. But it would seem on closer examination that all these changes were superficial. Deep under, the inherent traits and character acquired over the centuries persist.   *The Malay Dilemma*, 1970

ॐ

There is little doubt that Malays were exclusively involved in marketing, petty trading, importing and exporting and even manufacturing in the early Malay sultanates. There were skilled Malay craftsmen, artisans and skilled labourers. Except for a much smaller population and a more limited area, economic life went on very much the way it now goes on despite the fact that there were no Chinese.   *The Malay Dilemma*, 1970

The influence of Islam on the Malays was tremendous. The Arabic language and culture which are part and parcel of Islam were absorbed by the Malays and caused drastic changes in their way of life. Adaptation of the Arabic script by Malay scholars resulted in increased literacy and an easier acquisition of the philosophy and sciences of the Middle East. Unfortunately, all the cultural and educational changes brought about by Islam remained for the most part in the town areas. Later on, when teachers moved into and established religious schools in the rural areas, their teaching was limited to religion only. Philosophy and the sciences did not find ready acceptance. The influence of custom or *adat*[10] and the strong animist beliefs of the rural areas limited Islamic teachings, and caused the practice of Islam to merge with Malay adat and its animist basis.   *The Malay Dilemma,* 1970

ૐ

Merdeka brought power and wealth to the new Malay elite. The trials and tribulations of the war and immediate post-war years were over. Politics was found to be the panacea. It provided a short-cut to everything. It made possible the attainment of positions of immense power. It brought about laws and policies that placed some Malays in a position to acquire great wealth, or at least a good livelihood without trying too hard. It made life in the kampongs more comfortable and less isolated from the towns. In other words, politics created for the Malays a soft environment which removed all challenge to their survival and progress.   *The Malay Dilemma,* 1970

ૐ

What is considered as Malay culture or way of life, even in the days before Independence, carried many alien traits. Malay language, attire, food, customs and so on have gone through a process of change, assimilating foreign elements along the way. Hindu and Islamic influences, though dominant, are but two features. One can only go through Bahasa Malaysia dictionaries to see that Malays have adopted words from all over, not confined to Sanskrit and Arabic.   *Universiti Malaya, Kuala Lumpur,* 1983

In the social field, Malays always isolate themselves. In the course of this, we cannot influence anyone. We prefer to use our power to get cooperation rather than use friendliness fo the same purpose. To succeed in politics, social field and economy, interaction with other races is an important factor.

UMNO General Assembly, Kuala Lumpur, 1987

੩▲

A small group of Malays has achieved wealth purely from business with the government. Without the government, Malays cannot compete. This is not the achievement we want and hoped for in the New Economic Policy.

UMNO General Assembly, Kuala Lumpur, 1987

੩▲

The culture which prevailed when Prophet Muhammad brought Islam to the Arabs had already been ignored by most Muslims. Brotherhood in Islam is no longer practised by the Muslims. Everywhere they are at loggerheads with each other and are willing to collaborate with the enemies of Islam to defeat their fellow Muslims. In Malaysia this has begun to happen.

UMNO General Assembly, Kuala Lumpur, 2000

੩▲

There are Malays who allow themselves to be influenced by the enemies of Islam, so that the efforts to develop and regain the glory of the Malays and Islamic civilisation could be prevented.

UMNO General Assembly, Kuala Lumpur, 2000

੩▲

If changes in Malay culture result in gradual deterioration, then steps must be taken to create and instil a new culture that can resist temptations and overcome challenges of being rich urban Malays.

UMNO General Assembly, Kuala Lumpur, 2000

ON THE
NEW ECONOMIC POLICY

Our political enemies try to create doubts about the New Economic Policy[11] [NEP] which, according to them, brings benefits to only a few of the Malays. These people allege that the Malays who benefit from the NEP are friends of the UMNO leadership, particularly my friends.

Selangor UMNO Convention, Shah Alam,1983

One foreign newspaper said 'The New Economic Policy set up in 1970 ... has succeeded largely in discouraging foreign investments.' This piece of nonsense is probably the result of wishful thinking. This newspaper for some unknown reason finds it impossible to say anything good about Malaysia. It is alleged that this is a business newspaper. It reads *The News of the World*.

EMF Foundation Round Table, Kuala Lumpur, 1986

It was UMNO which came up with the New Economic Policy, a policy to restructure the economy so as to give the Malays and other Bumiputeras a fair share of the economic cake. Where others would have played Robin Hood and expropriated the wealth of the Chinese in order to distribute to the Malays, UMNO decided that the enhancing of the wealth of the Malays must come through enlarging the economic cake and distributing the enlarged portion more to the Malays while apportioning some also to the Chinese and Indians.

Malaysia in the New Millenium Conference, London, 2000

The NDP [National Development Policy[12]] contributed towards strengthening Malaysia's position as a modern industrial economy and brought significant economic and social progress. The country witnessed improving standards of living and the strengthening and diversification of its industrial base.

Parliament House, Kuala Lumpur, 2001

The National Vision Policy[13] maintains the basic two-pronged strategy of the New Economic Policy, that is, poverty eradication irrespective of race and restructuring of society in the context of rapid economic growth.

Parliament House, Kuala Lumpur, 2001

ॐ

While incorporating the key strategies of previous policies, such as the New Economic Policy and National Development Policy, the new dimensions of the National Vision Policy are as follows: developing Malaysia into a knowledge-based society; generating endogenously-driven growth through strengthening domestic investment and developing national capability while continuing to attract foreign direct investment (FDI) in strategic areas; increasing the dynamism of agriculture, manufacturing, and services sectors through greater infusion of knowledge; addressing pockets of poverty in remote areas and among Orang Asli and Bumiputera minorities in Sabah and Sarawak.

Parliament House, Kuala Lumpur, 2001

ॐ

The NEP has been on now for almost 40 years, far longer than originally planned. Admittedly the Malays had been at fault because they did not make correct use of the opportunities created for them in the NEP. But whatever the reason, the Malays have not gained for themselves the 30 percent target in corporate ownership even. But more than that, if a proper audit is made, their wealth is even less than 30 percent of total wealth of the people of Malaysia. Most of the wealth of the country belongs to the Chinese. It can also be said that the Chinese control the economy of the country. In the political field, the Malays appear to be in control. Most of the high posts, i.e. PM, MB, etc. are held by the Malays. If these posts are held by the Chinese, then not only will the economy be under Chinese control but the political arena would also be under the Chinese. What will be the Malay stake in the country? The NEP is about giving the Malays a fair stake in the economy of the country. Should they get this, then they should be ready to relinquish a commensurate amount of control in the political field. Since they have not gained a fair share in the economy, then they should be allowed to retain this greater share in politics.

Chedet.cc blog, 2010

ON ECONOMICS
AND DEVELOPMENT

If a nation, giddy with the glory of a newly won independence, nationalises foreign industries and refuses to pay compensation, the concerned investors will let out a mighty wail. They don't mind, they say, nationalisation. That is the right and the prerogative of independent nations, they say. But they do object to the failure to pay compensation, they say, even if inadequately.

Conference on Business in Southeast Asia, Kuala Lumpur, 1977

૨●

It is a fact that rapid development need not necessarily constitute orderly change and that planned change need not necessarily result in the expected. Development and change are a result of many inter-related factors. Some of these factors are unknown to us and some others are still beyond our adequate understanding. Development, which is a dream of all countries, therefore has a dimension of uncertainty and risk.

The Inauguration of the United Nations Asian and Pacific Development Centre,
Kuala Lumpur, 1981

૨●

We must substantially improve our productivity on a national scale.

National Seminar on Productivity, Kuala Lumpur, 1982

૨●

These are troubled times: not only have we to contend with a major world-wide economic recession, but also serious challenges to the peace and stability of our region. *Official Dinner hosted by the Prime Minister of Thailand, Bangkok, 1982*

Past experience has shown that inflows of long-term foreign capital, while important in helping to finance the required imports of capital goods and in attracting foreign know-how and technology, cannot be relied upon to finance significantly the investment and development process in our countries. Indeed, they are not a reliable source of funds; often, they are not forthcoming when you need them most. The 1981 World Development Report of the World Bank states that foreign capital financed less than one-seventh of the total investment in the non-OPEC developing countries in 1975–78. The limited role of foreign investment should drive home the point. It brings to the forefront a fact of life, that despite the talk and widespread publicity on foreign assistance, be they official development aid or foreign direct investment, we have all along been depending on ourselves. In a sense, we have within our control, the nucleus of both the means and the capacity to guide the destiny of our economies in the new world environment.

International Symposium, Kuala Lumpur, 1982

ह⋅

Although we have a sizeable manufacturing industry, [...] if we analyse the situation, we will find that to a large extent we are no more than sub-contractors. Either we manufacture components or small sub-assemblies for export and incorporation into completed products, or we import components or sub-assemblies and merely assemble them here. We only have to look at such industries as motor vehicles [to be] certain that we have the talent necessary to tackle the problem but I am equally certain that we do not yet have the correct attitude to do so. *National Seminar on Productivity, Kuala Lumpur, 1982*

ह⋅

Malaysia is undergoing a fairly rapid rate of development and modernisation. While we need the cooperation of the advanced countries to boost our economic growth, we also place considerable emphasis on self-reliance. The harnessing of scientific and technological knowledge is vital to that self-reliance. We are not about to invent the wheel again but the application of discoveries and inventions originating elsewhere is a part of the exercise in self-reliance. Of course we intend to fully utilise all the foreign expertise that may be made available to us.

Meeting of the Commonwealth Science Council, Kuala Lumpur, 1982

In our endeavour to satisfy needs, people have become more and more materialistic in their mental outlook and conduct of daily affairs. The ringgit assumes undue importance and everyday considerations are linked to how to get more ringgit. If this goes on, it is likely that the individual will forget or lose the human values of affection, kindness, consideration and love for God. Before the 'ugly and money-minded Malaysian' image comes to us, our schools, colleges and religious institutions must play a decisive role in moulding Malaysians to be disciplined morally and spiritually. National development must have as its parallel, spiritual and moral development.

National Seminar on Productivity, Kuala Lumpur, 1982

ॐ

Our patience and sense of fair play is being taxed to the limit with the market manipulations abroad which in effect reduce our people to underpaid labourers. As a producer of primary commodities like tin, rubber and palm oil we are as much entitled to a fair return on our outlay as any producer of manufactured goods in the developed countries. Producing these primary products is no longer merely a question of having enough land or minerals and cheap labour. While the manufactured goods that we buy are priced according to the cost of production and marketing and of course a hefty profit, the prices of primary products seem to bear no relation to any of these costs. They are priced according to the whims and fancies of a host of people who have nothing to do with their production.

United Nations General Assembly, New York, 1982

ॐ

Commodity prices today are at their lowest. We can blame the recession for this. But what we regret is that this recession is man-made. There is no shortage of supply, nor is there a shortage of demand. Energy is plentiful and the level of technology is unprecedented. Yet suddenly no one wants to buy what only yesterday they could not have enough of. And those who want to buy are without the necessary foreign exchange. Indeed many poor countries have literally to sell their soul in order merely to survive.

United Nations General Assembly, New York, 1982

Such is the fate of the producers of primary commodities that they now have to sell three to five times more of their produce in order to buy the same amount of manufactured goods from the developed countries as they did 20 years ago. In other words the gap between rich and poor has widened by 300 to 500 percent in the last 20 years or so. Malaysia is trying to break the vicious circle of the old commodity market system. We are trying to set up a more equitable system which will maintain reasonable prices while ensuring adequate supply of tin and rubber to the world. Towards this end we have tried to form a viable and effective producers' association. There is no intention to create a monopolistic situation. We know fully well that unreasonableness on our part will result in reduced consumption and a switch to substitutes. We hope that producer countries everywhere will appreciate the need for this strategy and participate in it.

United Nations General Assembly, New York, 1982

The developing countries are being persuaded more and more to buy and put up plants which produce manufactured commodities in excessive quantities. The plant fabricators make a lot of money up front while excessive production ensures that the particular commodity floods the market with the expected results.   *Meeting of the ASEAN Economic Ministers, Kuala Lumpur, 1985*

Our emphasis now is on wealth creation rather than wealth distribution. We are sure we can manage our social engineering when the economy recovers.   *American International Group Investment Seminar, Kuala Lumpur, 1986*

Malaysia is not teeming with entrepreneurs and good managers. We cannot annihilate the few that we have. We have to give them a chance. Not to all, of course. But those of them who show initiative and who honestly try to repay when they can – they should be helped. They should not have the carpet pulled from under their feet.

Annual Gathering of Financial Institutions, Kuala Lumpur, 1986

The government is prepared to spend to develop the country in the interest of all people.   *Opening of the Kota Kinabalu International Airport New Terminal, 1986*

ና▲

If today we are not doing so well economically, it is not because we have lost the knack of managing our multiracial country with its myriad [...] problems, but it is because outside forces have depressed the prices of our commodities, and played havoc with our exchange rates. We will overcome nevertheless. The EMF's [European Monetary Fund's] decision to hold its meeting here is to us a vote of confidence in this country but compare what you read with what you see when you come here, better still compare this country with other countries that you know. Countries that are badly administered tend to show physical evidence of this failure: dilapidated roads, buildings, vehicles, public facilities, etc. will in one way or another reflect the failures of an administration. But in Malaysia, a developing country with a per capita income one-fifth that of developed countries, do you see these physical evidence of corruption, instability, inefficiency, etc.? I will not answer this for you. There will be ample time for you to make honest assessments of this country. Then I am sure you will not rely too much on what you read about faraway lands.   *EMF Foundation Round Table, Kuala Lumpur, 1986*

ና▲

The Malaysian government believes that it must work closely with the private sector in order to facilitate business. We have coined the term Malaysia Incorporated to describe this close [relationship]. Admittedly it is not very original but it has helped the bureaucracy and the business community to change their attitudes toward each other. You can invoke this concept should you find problems in dealing with the bureaucrats.

American International Group Investment Seminar, Kuala Lumpur, 1986

We produce the chips in American-owned factories in Malaysia and they eventually end up in American-made computers which we buy at a fantastic rate so that Malaysia is now the third biggest user of computers in the whole of Asia. It is short-sighted for some quarters to say that Americans should invest at home only. Indeed it is short-sighted to say that America should restrict imports. If you deprive other countries of their foreign exchange earnings, how do they buy the products that you must export, however big your domestic market may be? How do they pay their debts to American bankers? *American International Group Investment Seminar, Kuala Lumpur, 1986*

ﻉ

National development results from the self-development of every citizen.
Scouts and Youth Leadership Camp, Rawang, 1987

ﻉ

We have been buffetted by numerous economic storms and pressures in the last few years. The resulting setbacks have shocked us out of our complacent view that growth is a function of time. We now realise that wealth creation needs entrepreneurship, management skill and greater productivity. It is because of this that we need to learn from the successful countries of the East. *Dinner hosted by Margaret Thatcher, London, 1987*

ﻉ

Since three years ago, we have tried to repair the country's financial position. We no longer borrow without taking into account the burden of the repayments. We have reduced government expenditure which in the past [was] very high. We have also tried to reduce the burden of paying salaries to civil servants by privatising some of the departments which the government feels it should not manage. *UMNO General Assembly, Kuala Lumpur, 1987*

When the commodity prices collapsed across the board with the Composite Commodity Index falling by 10 percent in 1985 and by another 24 percent the following year, the economy went into a tailspin. The economic growth turned negative for the first time since Independence. We thought that diversification or 'not putting all our eggs in one basket' was a good strategy but no one expected all the baskets to fall crashing at the same time.

Official Opening of Bank Negara Malaysia, London, 1989

Our competitive edge will come from our comparative advantage in natural resources and our productive labour force. We encourage flexibility in wage determination and a wage structure which encourages productivity in order to remain competitive internationally. What is important is the continuing need to inculcate a healthy work ethic and a positive attitude to nurture the growth of rising productivity. Only in this way can Malaysia maintain its competitiveness, independent of movements in the exchange rate.

World Economic Forum National Meeting on Malaysia, Kuala Lumpur, 1989

We do not want to be an NIC [Newly Industrialised Country] because we think there should be no such term. There should be no such categorisation and there should be no such discrimination. We do not need the title. Every country should be free to grow economically and be as rich as the richest or richer still. For, so long as there is no unfair trading practices, countries should be left alone to develop. Already Malaysia has been invited to conferences of the NIC's, the near NIC's and the developed countries. We have refused to attend. We see in this an attempt to categorise us and to penalise us for our economic performance. We see in the NIC a ruse to stifle our progress. The problem is that many Malaysians are very anxious to be called an NIC. If we accept the label, then we must accept the strictures that go with it. Why are we doing this to ourselves? Can I call upon fellow Malaysians to refuse the label NIC? We are interested in growing but they can keep the title and what goes with it. We are going to protest about the unfairness of this categorisation as NIC.

Convention of the Malaysian Economic Association, Kuala Lumpur, 1989

Over the long haul, the government is neither a sustainable nor an efficient source of stimulus to growth. The reliable 'engine' is private initiative. Government should play the catalytic role in promoting and inducing private sector activity. It should provide the basic infrastructure facilities, and the stable political and financial environment to nurture the growth of long-term real investments.

World Economic Forum National Meeting on Malaysia, Kuala Lumpur, 1989

෫ඞ

By any measure Malaysia has done very well. The government would like to claim that we are the sole cause of the remarkable economic recovery and performance. But we would like to admit though, that government policies and directions alone would not achieve results. It would be like clapping with one hand. I am not saying this out of modesty. It is to avoid and to discourage 'the government should do something' kind of mentality. The government can do something but the various sectors of the economy must do something also, or at least, respond positively to government policies and initiatives.

Annual Dinner of Financial Institutions, Kuala Lumpur, 1990

෫ඞ

We need people who are good at making money; the more their money, the more taxes they pay to the government.   *Jitra, Kedah, 1993*

෫ඞ

Malaysia's success in attaining and sustaining the competitiveness of its exports has resulted in Malaysia being regarded as one of the industrialising countries deserving coverage in the World Competitiveness Report. Our current high ranking in that group, behind Singapore, Hong Kong and Taiwan and better than some of other dynamic countries of the East Asian region, no doubt is a source of pride to Malaysians. It is also a big challenge for we attract the attention not only of those who wish to take advantage of our competitiveness but also those who wish to reduce our competitiveness.

First National Competitiveness Forum, Kuala Lumpur, 1993

I believe that the markets, and here I do not mean a few ultra-rich capitalists in a developed country, when well regulated and prudently supervised, whether domestically or globally, can be an enormous force for social good. Much of our own Vision 2020[14] is dependent upon the exertions and creative energies of individuals and enterprises.

Prime Ministerial Lecture of the Harvard Club, Kuala Lumpur, 1998

ð

I have been blessed with the opportunity to be part of Malaysia's growth – seeing its transformation from an agriculture-based economy to one focused on manufacturing. A key success factor in this progress was our emphasis on becoming globally competitive by creating a conducive business environment. Indeed our oil palm industry, as represented by the palms which you still see around us, still continues to lead the world. This tradition of global competitiveness continued into our industrialisation phase so much so that today, we are the world's largest exporter of microchips.

Official Opening of Cyberjaya, 1999

ð

Too often, the faceless economists of the world look at the economics of national development as though it is a phenomenon involving figures which measure material achievements without any relation to the welfare of people. They measure failures or success through GDP growth, per capita incomes, the profitability of corporations and, above all, the indices of the stock markets. Human welfare cannot be engendered if economics does not have a human face. The jargon of economics must change. Economics must be about people, their well-being, the benefits they derive, their joys and their sorrows, their health and their sickness, the peace and the freedom they enjoy.

Africa–Asia Business Forum, Kuala Lumpur, 1999

Let me be clear about what many have called 'the new economy' and 'the K-economy'. This is especially necessary because there has been a surplus of vague words, wonderful jargon, novelistic concepts and bombastic verbiage which only confound rather than clarify. Malaysia's 'Strategic Initiative One', the second step on which we are now embarked, does not mean the abandonment of our industrial backbone, which today contributes more than 37 percent of our Gross Domestic Product, which provides 30 percent of all jobs.   *Second World Knowledge Conference, Kuala Lumpur, 2000*

৵

Having dealt with equitable sharing and achieved political stability, Malaysia and the Malaysian people are able to press on with developing the country. I think we have done quite well there too. No extreme or radical approaches or policies were adopted. We could have nationalised everything, but we did not. We could have allowed for rampant capitalism but we did not. Instead we tried an odd mixture of state enterprises and free marketeering. When state enterprises failed, we easily privatised them. There was no ideological baggage to hamper us.   *Malaysia in the New Millenium Conference, London 2000*

৵

We are among the most industrialised [economies] on earth and we are not going to fall down the industrial ladder, no matter how many will try to push or pull us off. We are also one of the most open economies in the world. We live and we die on trade.

Second World Knowledge Conference, Kuala Lumpur, 2000

৵

It is sad that in this day and age, we should still find countries and people who are extremely poor while some countries are so wastefully rich. Yet there is so much talk about human rights and social justice. If wealth is more equitably distributed, then problems like child labour and sweat shops would not arise.

Confederation of German Industries and German–Asia Meeting, Berlin, 2002

It is time that the excessive wealth of the rich be subjected to a world tax in order to pay for needed infrastructure in the poor countries. It has been proven that construction and operations of public utilities not only cause an inflow of funds but act as catalysts for the development of a country.

Confederation of German Industries and German–Asia Meeting, Berlin, 2002

੨੪

Despite aiming only for job creation, Malaysia gained a lot more from the foreign investments in manufacturing. Its workers became highly skilled and commanded better pay. Some rose in rank and could take over the management. Some were able to design new products. Others acquired enough skills so that they could work for local companies and produce many of the components and even the final products.

Bangladesh–Malaysia Business Forum, Dhaka, Bangladesh, 2004

੨੪

The great banks are collapsing like a house of cards and rich countries are going bankrupt. And we all ask why. Why? It began with the delinking of money from gold. It began with fiat money. Basically these are paper tokens, with no intrinsic value at all. We never question how these pieces of paper can have a value. We never ask who has been printing these notes. We do not ask how the printers determine how much notes they should print. We all merely accept them as money.

Perbadanan Putrajaya, 2008

੨੪

Rating agencies wield power and, as they say, power corrupts. We should take their ratings with a grain of salt. We must be told the real basis for their ratings. Otherwise we may suffer the same fate as the Europeans and the Americans.

Chedet.cc blog, 2010

There is no way we can continue to enjoy [a] low cost of living while we ensure we earn high incomes. A high-income economy must therefore also be a high-cost (of living) country. But with good management the high incomes would increase our purchasing power to some extent, especially in the purchase of imported goods and services and when travelling abroad. There should be also a certain increase in purchasing power in the country. In effect despite higher cost of living we will still enjoy higher purchasing power and a higher standard of living. I am all for the government's high-income policy. My worry is that the people may expect high income without the accompanying high cost of living. It is better for them to be forewarned.

Chedet.cc blog, 2010

ะ&.

In Britain the highways are toll free. The government financed the constructions and maintenance of the roads through tax on petrol. The tax level is very high. The public pays more than twice the petrol price in Malaysia. The tax increases as petrol price increases. We rejected the idea of petrol tax for these reasons. Besides, people not using the highways would also have to pay. Toll payment means only users pay and they pay only for the length of the road they use. Petrol tax means non-users of the expressway would be subsidising the users, including commercial vehicles.

Putra World Trade Centre, Kuala Lumpur, 2011

ะ&.

QE II is not Queen Elizabeth the Second. It is a term invented in the West to describe printing money to pay debts or to revive the economy. It stands for Quantitative Easing No 2. It is a great way to make money to replace the money that a nation has lost in a recession caused by abuses of the financial system. You just print more money. Actually I don't think they actually print currency notes amounting to the hundreds of billions of dollars or pounds to replace the money they have lost [...] I suspect what they do is to issue cheques in favour of the banks. The amount would be entered in the books of the banks. However, this QE is a privilege for the rich nations only. When Greece lost money, it cannot print currency notes or issue cheques to pay debts. Greece needs to borrow money from European countries to repay loans.

Chedet.cc blog, 2012

Of the three elements of the government budget, only development spending can be reduced. Debt servicing and operations (salaries, pensions and other statutory expenditure) must be paid on time if we are not going to default. If we increase salaries too much, and we have more than a million government employees, there is a likelihood that we will not have enough for even minimal development. We may announce a big development budget but there will simply be not enough money to implement them. We may borrow. But there is a limit to borrowing. When you borrow the debt servicing charges will increase. A point will be reached when we will not be able to service debts or pay the lender when the loans become mature. All these elementary things must be known to the government. So we will not become like Greece. But people do not seem to know about this. Demands for pay increases, for higher non-taxable pensions, for abolition of tolls (the government has to make up for the loss of revenue by toll concessionairs), more holidays, more subsidies, etc. will continue to be made. *Chedet.cc blog,* 2012

∂▲

If you want to go somewhere, you must determine the destination. We want our country to develop. The destination must obviously be the developed countries. The steps that have to be taken must be those which lead to the status of a developed country. Hence Vision 2020. *Chedet.cc blog,* 2012

ON GLOBALISATION
AND LIBERALISATION

Presently the focus is on globalisation. Technological advances is the excuse for doing away with the independence of nations and replacing it with interdependent nations. We are told through their propaganda machine that globalisation is an idea whose time has come and resistance would be futile.

South Summit, Havana, Cuba, 2000

੧੦

Globalisation has already shown signs of becoming a religion that tolerates no heresy. This is rather unfortunate, for globalisation, if properly interpreted and regulated, can bring about a great deal of wealth and benefit to the world, the rich as well as the poor. The important thing is to focus on the results rather than dogma. If the results are good, then by all means implement it as currently interpreted and practised, but if the results are bad for anyone, then globalisation must be reinterpreted and modified until the expected results are achieved.

South Summit, Havana, Cuba, 2000

੧੦

We believe in what we call smart partnerships. Poor people make poor customers. But when you enrich them, they can turn into good customers. When foreign companies began to invest in Malaysia, they made good profit. But they also created jobs and many spin-off effects. Malaysians and others in Southeast Asia began to have more spending money. And naturally they became a good market of foreign goods and services. With more investments and increasing prosperity, their imports increased rapidly. The result is a big attractive market where there was virtually none before.

Europe–Asia Businesss Summit, Kuala Lumpur, 2000

We talk glibly of this world without borders, of a globalised world resulting from the ease of communication. It seems that strategic location is now quite meaningless insofar as doing business internationally or even nationally is concerned.   *Europe–Asia Business Summit, Kuala Lumpur, 2000*

ॐ

Perhaps what I am saying reflects the alarmist in me. But whether I am right or wrong, we need to really examine these things called globalisation and the fantastic world of the Internet. I think they will affect the way we do business between Southeast Asia and Europe. We want to be efficient but we do want to see the faces and talk to the people we do business with.

Europe–Asia Business Summit, Kuala Lumpur, 2000

ॐ

We had welcomed globalisation believing that foreign capital, know-how, etc., could help our economies to grow. Then, in East Asia, the rogue currency traders demonstrated that simply by devaluing our currencies they can make the so-called East Asian Economic Tigers suddenly into meowing cats. Millions were thrown out of work and made destitute. The international institutions then moved in, ostensibly to help with loans but in reality to facilitate the takeover of the countries' economies and even politics.

South Summit, Havana Cuba, 2000

ॐ

The rich interpret globalisation as the right of capital to cross and re-cross borders at will. Capital is the new gunship of the rich. By coming in with short-term investments they create an illusion of wealth. Once that has happened, they merely have to pull out their capital in order to impoverish and weaken their victims and force them to submit to foreign dictates.

South Summit, Havana, Cuba, 2000

If globalisation implies integration of all countries into one single global entity, then why should it mean only the free flow of capital and capitalists across borders? Why should not workers, especially unemployed ones, move across borders freely? If money is capital for the rich, labour is the capital of the poor countries. They should be allowed to migrate to the rich countries, to compete for the jobs there just as the powerful corporations of the rich must be allowed to compete with their tiny counterparts in the poorer countries.

South Summit, Havana, Cuba, 2000

ॐ

Frankly speaking I am worried and frightened at the preparations being made by corporations in certain industries and business activities in order to take advantage of liberalisation and globalisation. I am referring to the mergers and acquisitions which are making big corporations even bigger. Now many of these corporations are financially more powerful than medium-sized countries.

Plenary Session of the United Nations Conference
Trade And Development, Bangkok, 2000

ॐ

It is a mistake to exclude the weak and the poor from participating in the formulation of globalisation. They have a great deal of experience. We have seen in the East how Foreign Direct Investment (FDI), technological transfers and opening up of the markets of the rich has resulted in the poor countries becoming enriched. We have also seen how nations can be made poor suddenly. Our experience can help shape a globalisation that benefits all. So let us in.

South Summit, Havana, Cuba, 2000

ॐ

There is today a great deal of 'globaloney' about 'globalisation', a word we so often use because we don't quite know what we are talking about. I have no doubt that it will be brought to an abrupt end by the multitudes of the world if rapacious, unbridled and unconscionable capitalism bereft of ethics, morality and caring rides roughshod over the welfare of people.

World Knowledge Conference, Kuala Lumpur, 2000

Globalisation should stress results rather than methods. Presently we are being told that globalisation must be espoused and practised even if it destroys us.   *South Summit, Havana, Cuba, 2000*

？▲

We live in a world in which there are not so many facts on globalisation and where there is so much globalisation nonsense. It is not so easy to think straight when there are so many corporate giants showing their teeth and so convincingly hiding their ambition at gobbling us all up.

World Economic Development Congress, Kuala Lumpur, 2001

？▲

We live in a world where we are up to our necks in global nonsense. It is entirely possible that 99.99 percent of the global manufacturers of the globalisation facts have an axe to grind, a vested interest to protect, salaries to increase, a belief system to foster and intolerant gods to satisfy.

World Economic Development Congress, Kuala Lumpur, 2001

？▲

There are winners and losers in the developing world. And there are winners and losers in the developed world. It is no accident that 58 percent of Americans say that they are opposed to globalisation.

World Economic Development Congress, Kuala Lumpur, 2001

Because of differing social welfare safety nets and different levels of poverty and wealth, the immediate negative consequence of globalisation in the rich countries for most is the loss of a job. The immediate negative consequence in the impoverished countries is the termination of the practice of eating, at least for a while.   *World Economic Development Congress, Kuala Lumpur, 2001*

？▲

Malaysia is not against globalisation. The opening of markets to trade and investment has contributed to Malaysia's own growth. Trade itself is a major consequence of globalisation and a major engine of growth for many countries.   *Confederation of German Industries and German–Asia Meeting, Berlin, 2002*

Malaysia remains committed to market liberalisation. However, market liberalisation and globalisation must not mean anarchy in which the colossal banks and corporations can ride roughshod over everyone in their quest for profit. Liberalisation should not mean total deregulation. Globalisation should not be for the sake of globalisation. It should be an instrument for the betterment of humankind. We have seen too many ideologies and systems which held great promise at first only to destroy countries and people instead.

Confederation of German Industries and German–Asia Meeting, Berlin, 2002

Globalisation is about economics, about economic management, economic development, economic strength and economic forces. If we fail to develop economically, we will go under, we will be dominated and will lose our independence even though not a single foreign soldier will step on our soil.

Meeting of Moroccan Islamic Intellectuals, Think Tanks and Parliamentarians,
Rabat, Morocco, 2002

ON MALAYSIA INCORPORATED

Japan's and South Korea's economic success stories are well known. One of the reasons for the success of these two countries is the close cooperation between the government and private enterprise. Nowhere is the cooperation more marked and telling than when competing in foreign markets. Every effort is made by the government to ensure the success of the country's exporter or contractor. Indeed so close is the cooperation that the competitors from other countries get the impression that there is no distinction between government and the private entrepreneurs concerned. They both seem to represent one entity dedicated to the success of the country. It was then that the term 'Japan Incorporated' was coined. The term was derisive and derogatory, but whatever one might say of the system, there is no doubt that it helped Japan, and later on Korea, to achieve the economic miracle that we see today.   *AIESEC Seminar on Malaysia Incorporated, Kuala Lumpur, 1983*

'Japan Incorporated' is an obvious model for a Malaysia that is desirous of joining the ranks of developed countries. There has always been close cooperation between the public and private sectors in Malaysia but active support on the part of the public sector to ensure the success of private enterprises and vice versa is not quite well developed. Indeed in some unfortunate instances a confrontational attitude is adopted to the detriment of both. It is with this background that the concept of 'Malaysia Incorporated' was introduced. The idea is to make clear the rationale for a special effort to be made for making public and private sector cooperation more meaningful and more productive. I believe we can make our development more successful by emphasising this strategy.

AIESEC Seminar on Malaysia Incorporated, Kuala Lumpur, 1983

The basis of Malaysia Incorporated is nothing more than a mental attitude, and an underlying approach for ensuring that the public sector and all its personnel regard the success of business, commercial and industrial enterprises as part of their nation's and their own success. In other words, we must understand that we have a stake in every economic undertaking operated by the private sector, as indeed, we are. If a private venture is successful, and can be more successful with all the assistance of the government, it will not only get more profit, which the government will also reap in the form of 40–55 percent taxes, but also it will generate more employment opportunities for our unemployed, and it will open new opportunities for other businesses, big and small. And since the government is also engaged in commercial and industrial enterprises, directly and indirectly, they too will benefit from better services provided by the public [and] everyone engaged productively – everyone having more purchasing power, consuming more, saving more and investing more. We will be stimulating and accelerating the whole growth process and wealth creation. As a bonus, everyone will be better disposed towards other members of the community.

AIESEC Seminar on Malaysia Incorporated, Kuala Lumpur, 1983

For the private sector people, they should not regard the civil servants as the people who are out to make their lives miserable, waiting to be buttered and so on.   *AIESEC Seminar on Malaysia Incorporated, Kuala Lumpur, 1983*

The Malaysia Incorporated concept simply institutionalised a natural relation between two important segments of society. There is no reason to regard this relation as improper. It may lead to corruption and cronyism, etc., but the confrontational approach to government/private sector relation can also lead to corruption and cronyism. When people have bad values, any system will lead to abuses. Blaming the system does not help resolve the problem. It is far better to try to tackle the abuses than to reject or condemn a system which can yield good results.   *Malaysia Incorporated Summit, Kuala Lumpur, 2000*

ON THE LOOK EAST POLICY

We are on the threshold of an era of great achievements in the various fields. We are looking towards those countries which are scientifically and technologically advanced. I have stressed the need to emulate certain aspects of work ethics of the Japanese and the Koreans and we are sending our people for training in the Republic of Korea and Japan. Our people will have to acquire new languages for this purpose and it is my sincere hope that all Malaysians will look at the new approach to learning positively so that we can look forward to reaping the fruits of progress and development instead of being used by those who would like to cause mischief and retard our progress and disrupt the unity and stability that we have.

Anniversary Dinner of Fei San Malaysia, Kuala Lumpur, 1982

If we in Malaysia want to achieve our goals, we must emulate the Japanese. I do not suggest for one moment that we should slavishly copy everything they do. I am fully aware that our climate is different, our environment is different, our culture is different. I do suggest, though, that we could learn a lot from the Japanese, particularly the work ethics that contribute to high productivity.

National Seminar on Productivity, Kuala Lumpur, 1982

Let me assure you that in adopting a 'Look East' policy in order to balance foreign influences on our national development, we are not turning our backs on the West completely. The West remains an important partner in our development efforts

Parliament House, Kuala Lumpur, 1982

The government is also encouraging the establishment of *sogo shosha*[15] and I am happy to note that at long last they are showing signs of taking off. Although it is not yet up to expectations, the establishment of such trading enterprises will surely help to promote more aggresive direct trading in our manufactured goods and commodities. It is the task of our *sogo shosha* to establish themselves as creditworthy and credible intermediaries in all transactions involving both exports and imports into Malaysia. They should help develop the kind of services that are presently being provided by foreign countries.

Annual Dinner of the National Chamber of Commerce and Industry, Kuala Lumpur, 1983

৵

We adopted a 'Look East Policy'. We had been looking west but the West had been industrialised a very long time and had forgotten how they dealt with the initial difficulties posed by industrialisation. The Japanese and Koreans had only very recently industrialised. They still remember their problems, their difficulties and how they overcame them. We could learn more from the Eastern countries than from the West.

Global Competitive Forum, Riyadh, Saudi Arabia, 2009

৵

In the West we found that there is built-in instability. The West believes in competition in the settlement of all disputes. The winner in the competition is considered to be in the right and the winner takes all.

Global Competitive Forum, Riyadh, Saudi Arabia, 2009

৵

Malaysia decided not just to look at the developed West, but more at the burgeoning economies of the East, principally Japan and South Korea. 'Look East' became Malaysia's slogan. It was not about industrialising as much as it was about acquiring the work ethics of these successful nations. I believe firmly that work ethics determine the success or otherwise of a nation.

Chedet.cc blog, 2012

ON CARS AND PROTON

I wonder how many of you have sweated in frustration in the traffic jams on the Federal Highway during the rush hour. Have you noticed the hold-ups that result from the major construction work that is going on at various points along the highway? No sooner do you clear one bottleneck before you meet the next one. The effect is cumulative and what starts as a traffic crawl ends up as a complete traffic standstill. The end result is a large number of people arriving late at their places of work, frustrated and in no condition to work efficiently. To this we can add the waste of fuel and additional pollution resulting from vehicles running while stationary. I commend the speed with which these projects are being carried out, but would not better planning and phasing of each stage of the work result in a reduction in the disruption at present being caused? *National Seminar on Productivity, Kuala Lumpur, 1982*

এ✿

It is not impossible for the Proton Saga to be the World No. 1 car.

EON Plant, Shah Alam, 1989

এ✿

The Proton Saga is a symbol that we are a dignified people, a people who are prepared to face challenges and people who will pick themselves up when they fall and overcome whatever obstacles and succeed.

EON Headquarters, Shah Alam, 1993

এ✿

We have a small automotive industry in Malaysia. Protected, we have survived. But left naked, we will be swallowed up, we will disappear. And with it goes not just our national pride, which is important to us, but also our design and engineering skills that we need in order to join the ranks of the developed nations. We do not want to be working for other people all the time. We want to be our own masters.

Regional Geo Economic Forum, Zagreb, Croatia, 2004

We expected our car to be as perfect and uniform as the saga seed, but to be frank, the standards of the first Proton Sagas were not really up to the mark.

A Doctor In The House, 2011

੩੦

There was a time when government protection of Proton was high that it won 80 percent of market share. Today it has only 26 percent of the market. If it goes down further, we may have to shut down Proton. This will not lower the prices for foreign cars. The government would still have to recover subsidy cost. But some 150,000 jobs generated by the national car industry will be lost. There will be a big outflow of foreign exchange to purchase imports. We will lose much of our engineering capability which in turn would lead to more job losses as engineering-based industries cannot fund skilled workers.

Chedet.cc blog, 2013

੩੦

The automobile industry requires big capital – usually in the billions of US dollars. This is so especially upon establishment. But Malaysia's national car had a capital of about RM400 million (about USD150 million). It borrowed from the government RM800 million. It has since paid back this loan fully from internal sources. Admittedly at the beginning it was not a roaring success despite lower prices. But at one time later on it commanded 80 percent of the local market and it built up reserves of RM4 billion. Since the beginning it paid directly and indirectly billions in revenue to the government.

Chedet.cc blog, 2013

੩੦

So why should we have an automotive industry? Well, let's look again at the contribution made by a national car industry. First it creates jobs, thousands of jobs not just in producing cars but also in producing components and parts. It enables Malaysia to acquire engineering knowhow. If the country is to become industrialised, it must acquire engineering skills such as designing, modelling, prototyping, testing, tweaking, upgrading and updating and a host of other things required for the manufacture of cars. These skills contribute to the industrial sector. It will qualify us to become a developed country.

Chedet.cc blog, 2013

We sell roughly 600,000 cars a year. Half the number would be local-made cars. Assuming an average price of RM40,000, the total sale value would be about RM12 billion. That would be the additional amount that will flow out if all cars are imported. It would certainly increase the deficit. The national cars clearly contribute much towards reducing our deficits.   *Chedet.cc blog,* 2013

ই৵

When the idea of a national car was mooted, it was met with widespread criticisms and cynical comments. We were a third-world country and we knew nothing about motorcar manufacturing. Our market was tiny. It would be a waste of our money [...] At best we could [...] assemble the cars here. That was as much as our agriculture-based economy could do. But we did talk even at that time of industrialisation, of being an industrial nation. How do we become an industrialised nation if we have no industry other than assembling electronic components?   *Chedet.cc blog,* 2013

ই৵

Of some interest are the so-called free-trade agreements [FTAs]. There is much focus on automobiles. Import duties are to be withdrawn for national cars of member countries. A car is regarded as national if it has 40 percent local content. Foreign car makers are quick to take advantages of this simple definition. They simply produce their cars in the member countries of the FTA with 40 percent of the cost incurred locally. With that they can access the markets of the FTA members and benefit from the tax-free status of national cars. One has to remember that these foreign cars have been sold in large numbers in the manufacturer's domestic market and in other countries. The cost of development would been amortised quickly so that even if the sale prices in the FTA countries are low, they would still be profitable. Proton's local content is 90 percent and its sale is largely in the local market where it has to compete with imports. Even with reduced taxes, it cannot sell well in FTA countries. The volume just cannot be big enough and it takes time to amortise the cost of development. In other words Proton is at a disadvantage in Malaysia and in the AFTA countries.   *Chedet.cc blog,* 2013

ON THE
ASIAN FINANCIAL CRISIS

The IMF has now admitted that it had made a 'slight mistake' in dealing with the Asian economies. It may be slight for the IMF but the cost to the countries of Asia is horrendous. Trillions of dollars of hard-earned assets and economic capacities have been destroyed, lost forever. In fact lives have been lost, governments have fallen and racial animosities intensified. The partnership between neighbouring countries has been undermined and regions destabilised. Clearly the result of the small mistake by the IMF is anything but small. It has destroyed the work of decades of a huge chunk of the world.

Prime Ministerial Lecture of the Harvard Club, Kuala Lumpur, 1998

The so-called creative destruction indulged by the powerful Western countries is not creative at all. Creative destruction is nothing more than an attempt to explain away a destructive self-serving act, an attempt to justify the unjustifiable. *Prime Ministerial Lecture of the Harvard Club, Kuala Lumpur, 1998*

When our currency plummeted and when our stock market plummeted, we quickly adopted, like the most obedient of sheep, all the prescribed measures. The Western press called this formula 'the IMF without the IMF' – massive increases in interest rates, massive cuts in government expenditures, massive contraction in credit. Then, like absolute idiots, we wondered why our currency was subjected to continued attack. And having cut off our lower legs, like absolute idiots, we wondered why our economy was dropping to its knees. *World Economic Forum, Singapore, 1999*

I am sure all of you know how currency trading is done but I have to relate the process because people talk of devaluation as if currencies have sensors and can detect when the governments are corrupt, nepotistic, etc. When they do they seemingly devalue themselves. You know they don't. Some people do that and the people are the currency traders out to make fortunes for their rich investors.   *Asia Society Dinner, New York, 1999*

৵

Clearly the currency traders can attack any of the developing countries, especially those which are doing well like the so-called 'Asian Tigers'. It was not their weakness which precipitated the attacks. Observers must notice that they never attack poor countries, however weak their finances may be. It is not because they are being kind, but because there is no money to be made.
                                             Asia Society Dinner, New York, 1999

৵

The financial turmoil had already undone most of the success of the affirmative action. The IMF in its usual uncaring way would worsen the situation further. And there would then be race riots and prolonged political instability. Then the foreign investors would not come in because they would all be flying to quality, i.e. to Russia and Latin America where there is a lot to be made by undermining the economies of these nations.
                                             Asia Society Dinner, New York, 1999

৵

When we imposed controls, we were vilified and condemned by practically the whole world. We were told our economy would be shattered as a black market in foreign currency would undermine our controls. We were called pariahs, idiots with no understanding of economics and finance. Now the comments are kinder. Even our most virulent critics have admitted that we have succeeded in overcoming our economic problems, that we are growing again. Some even project better growth than we do.
                                             Asia Society Dinner, New York, 1999

Now we are being advised to lift controls as we are now stable. We are not about to do so, not unless the world curbs the currency traders and designs an international financial structure that is less liable to [be abused] by the avaricious. I am trained as a medical doctor. I not only have to cure my patients but also to advise them not to expose themselves to a recurrence of the disease if possible. The currency traders, the highly leveraged funds and the possibility of their attacking us is still there. We will not lift our selective controls until the threat is removed.   *Asia Society Dinner, New York, 1999*

꙳

We are doing quite well and we are not doing any harm to anyone other than the currency manipulators. We only wish the world to know that there are many ways to skin a cat. The idea that there is only one way to tackle an economic problem is erroneous. So please leave us and our selective controls alone. What people think of us is not important to us. People have never thought well of us at any time. What is important to us is that we do well for our country and our people.   *Asia Society Dinner, New York, 1999*

꙳

The countries of East Asia continued with their own ways of growing their economies. It looked like there was no stopping them. They were going to grow and they were going to continue to challenge the West. There was a good chance for the 21st century to become the Asian Century. Again I would stress that there was no conspiracy. The attacks against the East Asian economies were not orchestrated. It is most likely that the rogue currency traders just saw an opportunity to make a pile for themselves. Be that as it may, the fact is that their attacks soon left most of the East Asian economic tigers in a state of unprecedented economic turmoil and sudden poverty. From being economic threats to the West, they suddenly found themselves totally dependent on the West for their recovery.

Asia Society Gala Forum, Hong Kong, 2000

The economic turmoil in East Asia has resulted in the rich taking what belongs to the poor. As the banks and businesses of the former Asian tigers collapse and as their share prices plunge, the rich have moved in to buy the devalued shares and acquire the companies. They could have bought at normal prices during normal times but they preferred to emasculate us before they take over at a fraction of the cost. Backing this move are the international institutions, which insist that we open up our countries so that the predators can move in to take over everything. Governments may not protect local businesses. Market forces must prevail and since money equals force in the market, those with money will dominate.   *South Summit, Havana, Cuba* 2000

≥▲

The truth of the matter is that at the beginning of the crisis, we did adopt policies similar to the IMF approach. We were told that the IMF policies of tight fiscal and monetary policies would restore market confidence and stability. Unfortunately, these policies not only did not restore confidence, but actually aggravated the crisis, as the reduction in government expenditure reinforced the contraction in domestic demand, while higher interest rates took their toll on the balance sheets of the corporate and banking sectors.

Cairo University, 2000

≥▲

Dangling the loan carrot and brandishing the big stick, the IMF, backed by the power of the powerful, demanded the dismantling of everything that had contributed to the amazing development of the East Asian tigers and dragons. Not only must corruption stop but subsidies for the poor, business-friendly governments, protective tariffs and non-tariff barriers, conditions on foreign ownership of businesses and banks, all had to stop. These countries must open up to direct and full foreign participation in their economies. There must be no restriction at all to foreigners wishing to take advantage of the business potential of the economies. Anything done to help local corporations in distress came under the general definition of bailing out cronies. These corporations must be forced into bankruptcy or sold to foreigners [...] That tens of thousands of poor workers would be thrown out of work as a result of the collapse of the businesses was irrelevant. Let them starve, riot and kill. But no government help should be extended.   *Asia Society Gala Forum, Hong Kong,* 2000

To cut a long story short, today the world admits that we were right about the rogue traders and we were right too in handling the crisis by imposing exchange rate controls and regulating short-term capital flows. Now our economy is back on track and growing much faster than the countries supposedly helped by the IMF and other international agencies.

Malaysia in the New Millenium Conference, London, 2000

❧

And so when disaster struck in 1997 and our currency was devalued, we did not have to rush for foreign help. The accusation that the turmoil was caused by the government being corrupt and practising cronyism, etc., did not hold water. If we were it could not have been only in 1997. We must have been corrupt, etc., for a long time. Yet our economy grew at a high rate and our development was rapid for years and years. It was not corruption, etc., but it was due to the currency traders selling down our ringgit in order to make money for themselves. When we condemned the currency traders for their greed, we were roundly castigated by the whole world.

Malaysia in the New Millenium Conference, London, 2000

❧

As a recalcitrant and heretic, I would like to insist that the affected economies of East Asia were practising the right economic policies, which enabled them to enjoy high rates of growth. Current account deficits and bank borrowings, which were on the high side, are to be expected given the openness of these economies and their high rate of economic growth.

Plenary Session of the United Nations Conference on Trade and Development, Bangkok, 2000

❧

Just as absolute freedom leads to anarchy, so too, 'absolute globalisation' could lead to chaos, as demonstrated by the recent financial crisis. We must avoid the tyranny of 'free markets', where power comes not from the barrel of a gun, but emanates from the chequebook. We do not subscribe to the view that market discipline is infallible, because markets have never been perfect and have a strong tendency to over-react and to be subjected to manipulations.

Cairo University, 2000

The propaganda machine of the West is good at making everyone feel guilty if he does not accept the new ideas and ideologies created by the rich to give them ever more advantage over the poor. Democracy, the free market, a world without borders, liberalism, etc., have all been cooked up in the rich countries and then forced on the poor. They all sound great but somehow their acceptance by the poor invariably destabilises them and puts them at the mercy of the rich. The free market is no more than a new name for Capitalism, unbridled Capitalism with a capital 'C'. The size of the capital involved today is unbelievable. It is said that the trade in currency, which is what capital is about, is said to be 20 times bigger than world trade. Such a huge sum of money cannot but disrupt businesses wherever it goes.

Cairo University, 2000

❧

It is time that we, the poor in particular, recognise that we are being led up the garden path by the sweet words and promises of new slogans, new systems and new ideologies. We recognise that we cannot go backwards but is it necessary that the way forward should be the one shown to us by the rich and the powerful?

Cairo University, 2000

❧

Despite accusations that the Malaysian government had indulged in wasteful projects to satisfy the prime minister's monumental ego, the fact is that we had managed our finances rather well. That is why when our ringgit was devalued we were still able to carry on. We had no foreign debts to pay. Indeed when Malaysia was down-rated by International Rating Agencies to prevent us from borrowing money, we simply used the vast amount of savings that we had in the country. Malaysia has perhaps the highest savings rate in the world – amounting to 38 percent of the GNP.

Malaysia in the New Millenium Conference, London, 2000

❧

Southeast Asia can recover faster and more strongly if it is less preoccupied with gaining the approval of the West in the way it manages things politically and economically.

Asia Society Gala Forum, Hong Kong, 2000

The attacks on the morality of Asian governments expanded to the other Asian economic tigers. All were accused of crony capitalism. The Asian governments were told they cheated by helping the establishment of corporate giants which were able to challenge Western supremacy in manufacturing, in commerce and trade. That these governments had built good economies, alleviated poverty and generally contributed to the well-being not only of their people but also of other people in the poor countries, meant nothing. These governments cheated by collaborating with their corporations and they must stop.

Asia Society Gala Forum, Hong Kong, 2000

ॐ

If we had mismanaged the country's finances, we would not be able to recover so quickly from the turmoil even if we [had imposed] exchange rate and capital flow controls.

Malaysia in the New Millenium Conference, London, 2000

ॐ

The instability in the global financial system has also adversely affected us. Although in the initial stages Malaysia found it necessary to follow the advice of the IMF, we had to abandon the IMF prescription because things actually got worse faster. We were thus compelled to adopt and implement measures consistent with our domestic circumstances in order to address the issues of economic recovery. These measures, although unorthodox, have helped to put the economy on a path to recovery.

Plenary Session of the United Nations Conference on Trade and Development, Bangkok, 2000

ॐ

Private investment was severely affected in 1998 as a result of the decline in demand and loss in investor confidence resulting from the financial crisis. To reduce the severity of the economic contraction, the government adopted a fiscal stimulus package and an accommodative monetary policy. Public investment focused on infrastructure development and enhancing productivity and efficiency to support private sector initiatives and fulfil the rising demand for better services from an increasingly sophisticated society.

Parliament House, Kuala Lumpur, 2001

In addition, the large inflow of foreign direct investment (FDI) into the manufacturing sector added capacity in the export-oriented industries, including the oil, gas and petrochemical sector and investments in capital-intensive and high technology areas, and contributed to the higher rate of private investment. The inflow of FDI remained steady even during the crisis.

Parliament House, Kuala Lumpur, 2001

èa

Exports were particularly crucial in propelling the recovery from the financial crisis. Exports grew at an average rate of 16.7 percent and became even stronger between 1998–2000. However, Malaysia emerged more resilient and fundamentally stronger after the crisis. The current account of the balance of payments turned around and strengthened following significant growth in merchandise exports. The merchandise account recorded the largest surplus ever of RM86.5 billion in 1999.

Parliament House, Kuala Lumpur, 2001

èa

From the onset, we have said that although we have a fixed exchange rate, we can fix it at any level we want. That is the most important thing [...] the freedom to fix the exchange rate.

Putrajaya, 2005

èa

I must admit that I am not trained in finance and not even in economics. I am a doctor of medicine. My little knowledge about finance and economy came through my serving as the prime minister of Malaysia during which time I had to handle many financial crisis, the worst of which was the 1997–98 currency crisis. To handle that crisis I had to ask a lot of economists and financial people a lot of questions and of course I had to read a lot on the subjects. However, not being from any economic school or financial institution, I was not constrained by the theories that are taught in such places. I could therefore strike out on my own and also do unorthodox things.

National School of Development, Beijing University, 2009

ON INTERNATIONAL TRADE

We have called for greater producers' cooperation to increase the negotiating power of developing countries and protect their legitimate rights. We have in this regard spearheaded the recently established Tin Producers' Association, and I am happy that the recent Non-Aligned Summit has recognised the importance of [the] Producers' Association. I would like to stress here that we are not in favour of cartels. To us the manipulation of prices by consumer countries constitute a part of a cartel operation. The Tin Producers' Association is therefore an anti-cartel organisation that is dedicated to free and fair trading in the commodity. We will never try to use the Association to hold the world to ransom. Rather we would work within the Association in order that the interest of the producers are as well protected as is that of the consumers.

Banquet in honour of Dr Mahathir Mohamad, Sri Lanka, 1983

ૐ

Allow me to touch on a persistent problem that Malaysia faces in the effort to improve her trade balance with industrialised countries. I am referring to the problem of trade barriers. Much of our effort to search for new markets are frustrated by tariffs, quotas and other restraints that hamper free trade. In many areas goods from countries like Malaysia do not provide competition for the higher technology goods from industrialised countries. Since free international trade is the vehicle of growth for all countries, Malaysia will always be in favour of dismantling trade barriers on a worldwide scale. Sweden's trade policy as well as its efforts to eliminate trade barriers within the context of GATT and UNCTAD is, therefore, especially welcomed and appreciated by us. *Dinner at the Residence of Swedish Prime Minister Olof Palme, 1985*

ૐ

The tradewinds that once brought your pioneer traders to the East in search of spices are now blowing in the reverse direction. We are now coming to your markets, to open the avenues of trade for our goods, just as we have opened our markets to your quality products.

Nordic Financial Institutions in Helsinki, Finland, 1985

A word about protectionism. It is the surest means to reduce world trade and impoverish the already poor. Thus markets will shrink not only for products of developing countries but those of developed countries as well. Poor countries cannot buy the capital and consumer products which they can never manufacture themselves. Reduced world trade in the end will impoverish all of us – i.e. the developed and the developing countries.

Asia-Pacific Council of American Chambers of Commerce Meeting, Kuala Lumpur, 1987

A disturbing trend is the assumption by the advanced industrial nations, the new Seven Sisters, of the role of regulators of the world's economy. Within the developed countries themselves, interest groups are forming effective blockades against imports of palm oil from developing countries for example. On a broader scale, regional trading blocs are also rapidly emerging. In North America, we have the free-trade pact between Canada and the United States. By 1992, a possible 'Fortress Europe' may emerge when the EEC forms a single European economic market bolstered by some form of financial union. And Eastern Europe might very well take a leaf from their western neighbours and form another European economic bloc. This trend towards polarisation will have far-reaching implications on economic behaviour worldwide, and may affect the economic survival of some.

Convention of the Malaysian Economic Association, Kuala Lumpur, 1989

You must excuse us if we continuously harp on [about] the possibility of Fortress Europe resulting from the unification of the European markets. Our fear is very real. Our market is so small that we will not be able to retaliate in any way. For many centuries we were the captive markets of European powers. Now that we have obediently accepted European free trade principles and we have benefitted a little from them, we find that the erstwhile protagonists are intending to switch to close systems. We are forced to ask ourselves whether in fact there is no such thing as neocolonialism or neoimperialism.

Official Opening of Bank Negara Malaysia, London, 1989

The terms of trade are not getting any better for the Third World. But now protectionism and unfair trading methods are creating havoc with the economies of the poor. While subsidies by the Third World may result in countervailing duties by the rich, they themselves subsidise their industries to the point where overproduction is encouraged and the markets become saturated. Consequently the products of the poor nations have become unsaleable. Surplus food is used to deprive poor countries of their markets.

Non-Aligned Movement, Belgrade, Yugoslavia, 1989

ट&

In view of the importance of international trade to the economy, Malaysia is committed to an open economic system and we wish to strengthen further our economic links with all our existing trading partners as well as develop new ones.

Brazilian Businessmen, Sao Paolo, Brazil, 1991

ट&

We want fair trade, not free trade for globalisation. Fair trade can be free but free trade can be unfair.

APEC Meeting, Bangkok, 2003

ट&

Before the coming of the Europeans in 1511, the Malay States of the Peninsula had traded with the Arabs, the Indians and the Chinese. We had no problems with these traders. But the European traders came in warships and demanded that we enter into trade treaties with them, allow them to put up fortified trading stations, and each country insisted on monopolies. Eventually they simply conquered us, making us their colonies so as to facilitate their trade. Today they are proposing that the world be globalised and borderless. They want trade to be absolutely free, to be regulated and disciplined by the market, meaning their banks, corporations and traders. With the past experience of trade with the Europeans, we would not be surprised if we end up by being their colonies.

Cairo University, 2005

We are a trading nation and for a trading nation the sufferings of its trading partners cannot but affect it adversely. We are going to find our trading partners unable to pay, partly because their banks are bankrupt and partly because their countries' recession must affect their buying power and their priorities when they buy. Our trade must therefore diminish and this will affect our industries and jobs for our workers. *Perbadanan Putrajaya, 2008*

Ever since the Europeans, and this includes the Americans, lost to the Eastern countries in the manufactured goods markets, they have switched to the financial market. Through the many products they created in this market, they seem to be able to grow and maintain their wealth and prosperity as shown by such indices as [...] GDP and per capita income. But the business is spurious. *Chedet.cc blog, 2012*

Oil drives the world. Ever since the invention of the internal combustion engine, the demand for oil has been increasing by leaps and bounds. Today the estimated total consumption of oil per day amounts to 70,000,000 plus barrels. Engines have been made more efficient, i.e. consume less oil for a given power. But still the demand for oil continues to rise. In 1973 the price of one barrel of crude oil was just USD3.50. The oil producing countries were being robbed. They remained poor and at the mercy of the Seven Sisters – the biggest and richest petroleum companies of the world. They dictated the price. And they paid royalty amounting to only 20 percent or so of the price of crude to the poor countries. The producing countries would have remained poor but for the anger over the state of Israel being supported by the West. Following the Yom Kippur War, the Organisation of Oil Producing Countries, decided to cut oil supply to the West. Suddenly the producer countries got the upper hand. They could deny supply and therefore they could dictate prices. Within one year the price shot up to USD12. From then on the price went up higher and higher. Today the price is USD120 per barrel. *Chedet.cc blog, 2012*

Malaysia has always been, and it still is, a trading nation. Buying things from foreign countries must result in outflow of funds. This would be bad for our balance of payment. Our trade would be in deficit. Trade deficits are not sustainable. We cannot generate enough wealth internally to pay for our imports. Our raw materials, such as rubber, tin and palm oil exports cannot earn us enough to pay for imports. We will be in deficit. To prevent this we can do two things. We can limit imports or we can increase exports. Among the items which absorb funds in large amounts is the import of cars. The purchase of cars involves large sums of money. When we buy foreign cars, there would be a big outflow of funds. In those days we could not think of exporting Malaysian-made cars in order to increase the inflow of funds and have a healthy trade balance. Still, if we produce our own cars and our people buy them, then much of the money would stay in the country. There would be less outflow, less tendency to have deficits. *Chedet.cc blog, 2013*

ON SINGAPORE

The development of Singapore and of Malaysia is a task not only of the leaders but the peoples of our two countries. Similarly, the development of good relationship between our two countries is also a task for the leaders as well as of the people. I will try, for my part, to ensure good people-to-people relations and I am sure this will be reciprocated.

Singapore, 1981

෭

I rejoice over the rapid progress and prosperity of Singapore because it also means that Malaysia will continue to have a happy and stable neighbour. An unhappy Singapore can be destabilising to Malaysia, likewise discontent in Malaysia can affect Singapore. Singapore leaders have spared no effort in developing the republic into a country with a united citizenry and similarly, we in Malaysia, have been moulding the country into a united and disciplined nation.

Singapore, 1981

෭

As a student in Singapore some 30 years ago, I made a lot of friends among Singaporeans who are now very prominent citizens of this republic. I can say that this experience is not unique to myself alone. There are many Malaysians who have shared similar experiences and have long-standing friends in Singapore, among them are some members of my delegation. So I cannot see any reason why what we do in Malaysia need earn the mistrust and suspicion of Singapore, and vice versa. We can always call up each other, and frankly discuss our mutual problems when they arise. Unfortunately, this connection of the old days in schools or universities is no longer possible among the new generations of Malaysians and Singaporeans. While it prevails, however, we should do our utmost to strengthen the foundation of good relations for the benefit of future generations of our two countries.

Singapore, 1981

The media has often been guilty of an inordinate amount of speculation on our bilateral relations, but this is only to be expected given the fact that Singapore and Malaysia were once one nation which separated because we had differences. It is natural to expect those differences to continue to haunt our relations.

Dinner in honour of Singaporean Prime Minister Goh Chok Tong, Kuala Lumpur, 1991

꿩

Malaysia will always consciously endeavour to understand the sensitivities and interests of Singapore and we are sure you would do the same. In a situation such as ours, where the scope of bilateral relations covers a wide range of issues, including those where our interests may not coincide, it becomes even more imperative that we consciously set out to work together. And in order that we can work together, it is necessary that we understand each other, avoid unwarranted suspicions, and establish close rapport.

Dinner in honour of Singaporean Prime Minister Goh Chok Tong, Kuala Lumpur, 1991

꿩

When we found that Singapore and its leadership were no longer compatible with the spirit of the federation and interracial tolerance, without much problem we gave Singapore its independence.

UMNO General Assembly, Kuala Lumpur, 2000

꿩

Singapore is Malaysia's neighbour. It is very prosperous though it produces practically nothing for export. It trades in Malaysian and Indonesian timber, palm oil, rubber, pepper, etc. It is able to do this because it is a free trader. Goods come in tax-free and are exported tax-free. Malaysia, Indonesia and the other Southeast Asian countries are not tax free. As a result people prefer to do business in Singapore with Singaporeans. Singapore's prosperity is not because it is tax-free. It is because its neighbours are not tax-free.

Regional Geoeconomic Forum, Zagreb, Croatia, 2004

We unfortunately have not been very good at claiming our rights. When we entered into agreements, we signed off what belonged to us so very easily, especially when we let treaties be valid 'for as long as there are stars, moon and sun'. We did not foresee that, in the future, people might want to be independent or want to change the conditions of the treaty. That is very bad. There must always be an 'exit' provision in any agreement so that [at] a certain stage in the future the treaty could be renegotiated or terminated.

Perdana Discourse Series 7, Perdana Leadership Foundation, Putrajaya, 2008

≈●

We were also careless when we drew up the agreement to supply water to Singapore. Of course as human beings ,we sympathise with the people of Singapore. We do not want them to die of thirst in Singapore. So way back in 1960, we were prepared to sell one thousand gallons of raw water to Singapore at three Malaysian cents (RM0.03) per gallon.

Perdana Discourse Series 7, Perdana Leadership Foundation, Putrajaya, 2008

≈●

We should be willing to supply the people of Singapore with raw water. The question is whether we should sell at 3 sen per 1,000 gallons and buy at 50 sen per 1,000 gallons of treated water as before, or we should extract better terms.

Chedet.cc blog, 2010

≈●

In 1963 Singapore joined the new state of Malaysia. The PAP did not believe in sharing power. It promoted meritocracy, rule by the elites, by suggesting that Malaysia was not ruled by the cleverest and the most qualified but by Malays. This was intended to stop Chinese support for the MCA and antagonise them against the Malays and UMNO. In the 1964 elections the PAP contested with the Malaysian Malaysia slogan to reflect its meritocratic creed. It won only one seat. The Chinese in the Peninsula, under the MCA rejected the PAP. The people of the Peninsula, in rejecting the PAP demonstrated their belief in the concept of *kongsi* or sharing espoused by the Alliance. Singapore and its chauvinistic meritocrats had to leave Malaysia. But a Trojan horse was left behind in the form of a political party named DAP.

Chedet.cc blog, 2013

ON ISRAEL AND PALESTINE

We remember vividly the horrors of Belsen, Dachau and other Nazi concentration camps of the Second World War. We know of the sufferings of the Jewish people then and the pogroms of centuries past. We were appalled at the atrocities. Nevertheless, nobody, not even a people who had suffered as much as the Jews had, have the right to inflict upon others the horrors of Sabra and Shatila. The Palestinians and the Lebanese were not responsible for Belsen or Dachau. Has the international community lost its conscience that it can stand aloof while such horrors were perpetrated against the helpless and the innocent? In order to assuage the conscience of the anti-Semites, the land of the Palestinians has already been taken away from them to create a Jewish homeland. Must the Palestinians now be butchered and driven from refuge to refuge? Must they also be exterminated?

United Nations General Assembly, New York, 1982

Israel is a bully. If it is any bigger or stronger, the world will not be safe. I would, therefore, like to call upon the United States, as the main supplier of weapons to Israel, to reconsider its position. Those weapons are for nothing less than murder. Apart from its systematic and premeditated use of lethal and sadistic weapons on occupied Palestine and Arab territories, Israel continues to propagate the myth of the non-existence of the Palestinian people and thereby frustrate all peaceful efforts to find a just and enduring settlement of the West Asian conflict.

United Nations General Assembly, New York, 1982

I wish to pay homage to the valiant Palestinian freedom fighters for their outstanding qualities of fortitude, patriotism and courage in the face of overwhelming odds in their just struggle for their inalienable rights. I also take this opportunity to salute Chairman Yasser Arafat for his statesmanship, foresightedness and courage in leaving Beirut in order to spare the civilian population of that city from continued Israeli savagery.

United Nations General Assembly, New York, 1982

The world and the supporters of Israel must prevail upon that habitually intransigent country to return to sanity and the ways of civilisation.

United Nations General Assembly, New York, 1982

❧

As Muslim countries we cannot but share the anguish of our brethren in West Asia. The repeated and blatant acts of aggression committed by Israel against the Arab people and their lands threaten regional security and world peace. We believe that a just and durable peace in the region can only be established on the basis of the restitution of the rights of the people of Palestine, including their right to set up an independent state of their own in their homeland under the leadership of their sole and legitimate representative, the PLO; the total Israeli withdrawal from all occupied Arab territories; and the unconditional return of Holy Jerusalem to Arab and Islamic sovereignty. We welcome the Eight-Point Declaration on the Middle-East peace settlement adopted at the Arab Summit in Fez in September 1982. Several months after the Israeli rape of Lebanon, they remain in occupation of parts of that country against the wishes of the people and government of Lebanon and the international community. It is about time that the United States government, the supplier of arms to Israel and on whose economic support Israel depends, apply the necessary pressure to effect immediate Israeli withdrawal from Lebanon.

Banquet given in honour of Dr Mahathir Mohamad, Nanday, Bangladesh, 1983

❧

Concerned as we are with issues directly affecting our regions, Malaysia has not and will not remain apathetic to threats to world peace emanating from other parts of the world. The plight of the Palestinian people comes immediately to mind. Long since uprooted from their own homeland, the Palestinian people have experienced untold sufferings and incalculable hardships for some 40 years. But that has not deterred them from pursuing their struggle to recover their just and legitimate rights so that they may have a home they can call their own. Malaysia will continue to support the Palestinian people for we believe no people must allow their sovereignty, their honour and their basic rights to be trampled upon.

Dinner in honour of Yugoslavian Prime Minister Milka Planinc, Kuala Lumpur, 1985

The animosity of the Arab Muslims towards the Europeans could have abated with their attainment of independence. Unfortunately the European powers left a festering sore which cannot be healed. While allowing the Arabs to regain their territories, the Europeans decided to make Palestine the homeland of the Jews, a project which would rid Europe of its Jewish problem. At the time when Palestine was made a Jewish state, there was only a small number of Jews living in peace with a huge majority of Arabs. Naturally the Arabs regarded the creation of Israel as an act of expropriating their land by the Europeans in order to appease the Jews and solve their Jewish problem. With this the seeds of future Arab violence against all that represent the Europeans were sown.

International Conference of Religious Studies, Kuala Lumpur, 1999

The world as we know it has forever been changed for the worse by the harrowing events of September 11. We risk our world plunging into more chaos as Israel seizes upon this event as an excuse to launch terror attacks against the Palestinians, claiming that it is fighting against terrorism. The result is predictable. Every time the Israelis attack, the Palestinians retaliate. Then the Israelis have to retaliate, which attracts Palestinian retaliation. There is not only no end to this but acts of terror are escalating and have already spread to other parts of the world. The attack against Iraq will simply anger more Muslims who see this as being anti-Muslim rather than anti-terror.

Opening of the Non-Aligned Movement's Business South–South Cooperation,
Kuala Lumpur, 2003

It was the British who proposed that the mandated territory of Palestine be established as a national home of the Jewish people and not to the people indigenous to the territory. It was an ill-thought-out decision for the British government must know that taking other people's land to give to other people is wrong, very wrong. They must have known it would lead to violence. They must have known that even when they occupied their colonial territories, they had been forced to give them up to the indigenous people. Palestine was not a piece of real estate owned by Lord Balfour or the British government, to be given away at their whims and fancy! There is no legal basis whatsoever, be it in English common law or the existing international laws, for this act. It was expropriation without parallel in history! What would the British people think if Surrey in England were to be offered by France or America as a homeland for the Jews, the Kurds or the Tamils of Sri Lanka and the people of Surrey be expelled?

Forum on Gaza Genocide, London, 2009

&

There may have been reference to Israel in the Bible but, even then, it was not as a nation state but actually as a vague part of Canaan. To claim exclusive right to a land based on some reference to it in a holy book is to legitimise all historical claims which will result in massive changes of the land and boundaries in the world. There would be endless conflicts and wars as there is hardly any country which does not have a historical claim to some territory or other. Even Malaysia has a lot of claims. Singapore was a part of Johore. But we realised the impracticality of claiming it.

Stability and Justice and Rights of Al-Quds and Palestine, Kuala Lumpur, 2010

&

One of the greatest injustices done was to take Palestinian land to give to the Jews to create the state of Israel. It was so easy to take what belongs to others in order to give to people who had been giving you problems in your own country. The Palestinians must be sacrificed to save the Europeans from the depradations of the Jews.

General Conference for the Support of Al-Quds, Kuala Lumpur, 2010

Until the creation of the state of Israel on Palestinian land, the world was secure for people to go about their business, to travel and to enjoy life. Now the security is gone. For the people who are responsible for the creation of the state of Israel, for the people who sustain it with their moral, financial and military support, there can be no security. The danger of being attacked or killed anywhere in the world will always be there.

Stability and Justice and Rights of Al-Quds and Palestine, Kuala Lumpur, 2010

≥№

Historically the Jews may have lived in the land that is Palestine. But historically the original people of America were the misnamed Red Indians, as were the Aborigines and Maoris of Australia and New Zealand. If all lands must be returned to the first people to live there, then return the United States, Latin America, Australia and New Zealand to the indigenous natives. But you won't, would you?

Chedet.cc blog, 2010

≥№

I am not anti-Semitic because I am not against the Arabs and other Semitic people or, for that matter, those Jews who reject Zionism. I am simply against injustice, against oppression and unmitigated and illegal violence. If that makes me anti-Semitic, then I am proud to be anti-Semitic, even though the term anti-Semitic is wrong.

Chedet.cc blog, 2010

≥№

Jews clearly cannot be condemned for anything because 60 years ago the Nazis of Germany committed atrocities against them. Apparently their sufferings of 60 years ago entitle them to [inflict] sufferings on the Palestinians whose land they had stolen. No matter how cruel or unjust they may be, no one may criticise them.

Chedet.cc blog, 2010

Today Israel is having problems with African immigrants running away from persecution in their own countries. Israel does not throw them into concentration camps but force them to live in the poorest section (ghettoes) of Tel Aviv. They were not allowed to earn a living. They were actually spat upon by Jews. Israel [tries] to expel them from Israel. They are offered $3,500 if they agree to be repatriated to their own countries. By all accounts these Africans are treated no better than the Jews living in the ghettoes of Europe before World War II.   *Chedet.cc blog,* 2014

ॐ

The Israeli prime minister, Benjamin Netanyahu, fears the possibility of African blood being mixed with Jewish blood. The Jews must remain pure. Seems that the Jews believe in racial purity. There is no difference then between the Nazis and the Israelis. Their oppression of the Palestinians is another indicator. Given power, Jews behave in the same way as the Nazis. Israel is truly an apartheid state. Only Jews can become Israelis. The Arabs of Israel are second class. As for the African immigrants, nothing would qualify them to become Israelis, not their adoption of the Hebrew language, nor their culture, nor their loyalty to the state of Israel. Jews condemned the German Nazis for the persecution of their people. Now they themselves are behaving like Nazis, persecuting the Africans.   *Chedet.cc blog,* 2014

ॐ

The world is required to sympathise with Jews because of the Holocaust. That is history. The world should judge the Israelis by their actions today.

Chedet.cc blog, 2014

ॐ

I think the whole world in the interest of justice should boycott doing business with Israel. This is truly a pariah state which is immoral and beyond the pale of human laws.   *Chedet.cc blog,* 2014

ON THE UNITED STATES

We think of the United States as a friendly country but domination by a friend is no more welcome than domination by an enemy.

Conferment of the Jawaharlal Nehru Award, New Delhi, 1996

୧**

Bereft of context, many might have agreed with the famous Samuel Johnson near the end of the 18th century when he said, perhaps only half jokingly, of the Americans that 'they are a race of convicts, and ought to be thankful for anything we allow them short of hanging'. Bereft of context, many in Europe might at the time have agreed with Robert Southey, who wrote in 1812: 'See what it is to have a nation to take its place among civilised states before it has either gentlemen or scholars. They (the Americans) have in the course of twenty years acquired a distinct national character for low, lying knavery.'

Luncheon at Council on Foreign Relations, New York, 1999

୧**

The unipolar world dominated by a democratic nation is leading the world to economic chaos, political anarchy, uncertainty and fear. We are not going to recover and have peace for as long as threats are used for political and economic reforms that most of the world is not ready for and not willing to accept.

United Nations General Assembly, New York, 2003

୧**

Other countries would have gone bankrupt with the twin deficits the United States suffers from. Although the United States has not, still the faith in the USD as a trading currency and as reserves has all but disappeared. The dollar is but a shadow of its former self. Once countries reject the USD as trading currency and as reserves, the greenback would become quite worthless. Unfortunately the countries, including Malaysia, which hold dollar reserves will lose also.

MAFAA Dialogue, Subang Jaya, 2008

Because of the extraordinary greed of American financiers and businessmen, they invent all kinds of ways to make huge sums of money. We cannot forget how in 1997–98 American hedge funds destroyed the economies of poor countries by manipulating their national currencies. When as a result of the so-called trade in currencies the companies in the poor countries faced bankruptcy, the governments were told not to bail out any company or bank which was in deep trouble. The Americans claimed that these companies or banks were inefficient and they should be allowed to go bankrupt and perish. Better still they should be sold at fire-sale price to American investors. Yet today we see the US government readying USD700 billion to brazenly bail out banks, mortgage companies and insurance companies.   *Chedet.cc blog, 2008*

ॐ

Desperate to avoid a serious recession, the US has abandoned all its principles. It has now banned short selling, limited currency trading and insists that the accounts of hedge funds and currency traders to be open for inspection and be published. In the final spasm of fear, the government has given itself the right to resolve the problem of bankrupt banks and companies by the government taking over, i.e. the great capitalist country has accepted what is nothing more than nationalisation which it had condemned so much before.

Chedet.cc blog, 2008

ॐ

The US's ability to threaten countries is undiminished. An attempt is being made even in Malaysia to achieve a regime change. Money has been funnelled to certain individuals and parties to ensure that a well-known candidate with extensive connection to the US Jewish lobby would somehow become the prime minister of Malaysia. US intervention in the politics of Malaysia is clear. I may not agree with the leadership of the present government but I resent and object to US manipulations to make a satellite of this nation.

Chedet.cc blog, 2008

The US now owes the world USD14 trillion. There is no way it can ever settle this debt. If other countries fail to repay or service their debts, the US would demand that they be made bankrupt. Now the US is literally bankrupt but it still insists that the pieces of paper, the famous or infamous greenbacks, have some value. It actually has no value. Certainly it cannot be used to finance wars of aggression against Iraq and Afghanistan, to finance the CIA (Central Intelligence Agency) activities in undermining governments and countries.

Chedet.cc blog, 2008

❧

In America, the greatest democracy in the history of mankind, Congressional and Senate lobbyists actually set up lobbying firms. Most of the firms' owners had been holding high positions in the previous governments and they know the staff and the members of the current government well. They openly offer lobbying service for a fee. If you don't have the money, that is too bad. The moneyed ones can actually cause motions to be put before the Congress which could be passed. In fact government policies in America have been shaped by the rich in Wall Street. I will not say more. Seems like those who take the moral high ground and criticise influence peddling in Malaysia and other developing countries should have a good look at themselves. Pots should not sneer at the blackness of the kettle.

Chedet.cc blog, 2010

❧

During my time Malaysia paid money to a lobbyist firm to lobby against the US' negative propaganda about palm oil for food. We had to do it on the basis of doing in Rome what the Romans do. We don't have this lobby system in Malaysia. If we have, I am quite sure we will be roundly condemned. But America is different. It can do just what it likes while taking the high ground to lecture to others.

Chedet.cc blog, 2013

ON WAR AND PEACE

Malaysia enjoys close and cordial relations with both Iran and Iraq, and we therefore implore them to cease fighting, accept mediation and reconciliation so that an honourable and an enduring solution can be found.

United Nations General Assembly, New York, 1983

ॐ

Our anguish is deepened by the continuing war between Iran and Iraq. The conflict between two brotherly countries not only endangers peace and stability but also undermines the solidarity of the Islamic countries, particularly in respect of the just struggle of the Palestinian people, the liberation of Holy Jerusalem and the valiant struggle of our Afghan Muslim brothers to preserve their faith, dignity and independence against Soviet intervention and occupation. We pledge our support to the peace efforts of the OIC for an early, just and durable solution of the conflict in the higher interest of Islam and for the stability and progress of the Islamic Ummah.

Banquet in honour of Dr Mahathir Mohamad, Nanday, Bangladesh, 1983

ॐ

Let me be perfectly plain and state that it would be insane for any Pacific state to be complacent about the existence of so much Soviet firepower in the region. At the same time, it would be mad for us in the region to live in a state of continuous fear and to die of fright. It is more reasonable for us to expect the Soviet Union not to use its military capability to directly aggress against any state in the Pacific, unless it is seriously or foolishly provoked. And there are no signs that any Pacific state has any irrational desire to indulge in the medieval sport of bear-baiting.   *International Monetary Conference, Hong Kong, 1985*

ॐ

If we are attacked, we ourselves will have to bear arms to defend our country. Other people will only sympathise and shed tears but will not help or go to war (on our behalf) unless it is to their gain.   *Kuala Lumpur, 1986*

The fact is that the major powers know nuclear war would wipe them both out. Yet they keep on building up their nuclear arsenal. Therefore, they spend until their economy is affected adversely and with this, the economy of the world. But the ones which really suffer are the developing countries like Malaysia.

UMNO General Assembly, Kuala Lumpur, 1987

ક્રી

The wars to end wars have been fought twice in the 20th century and have been won by the forces claiming to love peace. But we have never really been free from wars. Maybe not on the scale of the First and Second World War but for many countries and people the wars they have to experience, the wars of liberation and the wars to protect their freedom are no less fearsome and damaging. Thousands have died in Eastern Europe, the Middle East, in Central and South America, in East Asia and South Asia, and in Africa. For many, peace is still an elusive goal.

Asia Pacific Parliamentary Forum, Kuala Lumpur, 2003

ક્રી

I would like to have the Malaysian Armed Forces attack the United States and Israel. But I don't think the government and the MAF would agree with me. So what do we do? We could blockade the United States and deny it food and medicine. The blockade would have to go on for a hundred years. A lot of innocent people would die. But as Madeleine Albright said when asked whether killing 500,000 Iraqi babies was worth it, she said it was difficult but it was worth it. So Malaysians should not mind killing a few million Americans including babies because, although it will be difficult, it would be worth it. But I suspect we cannot blockade either. So what do we do? Let the bully do what it likes? But the bully is killing lots of innocent people together with small children and babies. But on the other hand, we need to drink Coca-Cola, use the Internet, fly Boeing jets, see Rambo movies, etc., etc. Can we sacrifice all these simply because babies are being decapitated by Israeli soldiers using highly sophisticated and costly weapons donated by the kind Americans? [...] If 10 percent of the people in the world who drink Coca-Cola stop drinking it, there would be some impact.

Chedet.cc blog, 2009

The Europeans also spend far too much on weapons. Research, development and upgrading swallow up huge amounts of money. As the weapons become more sophisticated, the costs go up sky high. Where before a fighter plane would cost a million dollars, now they cost 50 to 100 million dollars. Yet these weapons are quite useless in fighting the guerrilla wars they are likely to face. And they dare not have wars with countries with the same military capacities because it would be ruinous for everybody and would probably spell the end of the world. Their military budget contributes to the wastage of funds as the likelihood is that the weapons would never be used for the purpose they are developed, certainly not on the scale they are being prepared for.

Chedet.cc blog, 2012

ॐ

When in 1990 I first met Nelson Mandela upon his release, the first thing he asked was how Malaysia defeated the guerrillas. He said when he was being trained in Yugoslavia and Libya he was told that guerrillas could not be defeated. So how did Malaysia defeat the guerrillas? I explained that two things helped in the defeat of the Malaysian guerrillas. Firstly was the decision to move out all the people living at the fringe of the thick Malaysian jungle and locate them in protected new villages. Secondly was the campaign to win the hearts and minds of the people. Perhaps Jamalul Kiram[16] knows nothing about how Malaysia dealt with the guerrillas. His suggestion about conducting a guerrilla war in Malaysia seems to be based on ignorance. Yes, in the Philippines, the Moros conducted a guerrilla war for decades. While it harassed the Philippine government, it did not result in attaining independence for the south. In the end common sense prevailed and the MILF [Moro Islamic Liberation Front] decided on autonomy for the region. Malaysia followed the Moro fight very closely and is well aware that guerrillas can be disruptive. It can render Malaysia less stable and secure.

Chedet.cc blog, 2013

It looks like the Western powers have learnt something from their experience in Afghanistan and Iraq. They once thought that it would take only a few months of shock and awe to achieve regime change in these two countries. In the event after ten years of war, after losing thousands of their own soldiers while killing hundreds of thousands of Afghans and Iraqis, devastating these countries, the regime changes have not resulted in the democracy they expected. If at all, the present situation in these two countries is much worse than before invasion and the regime changes. The hesitation over a military adventure in Syria, even a limited one, is understandable. Yes, the use of chemical weapons probably killed over a thousand innocent Syrians. But already about 200,000 people have been killed. Is it acceptable to kill unlimited numbers of innocent people with bombs, rockets and bullets but not with chemical weapons?

Chedet.cc blog, 2013

෨

The soldiers and police who are currently participating in the fight against the terrorist in Lahad Datu are well-trained and well-equipped. The Malaysian forces have inherited the knowledge and the skills in fighting anti-guerrilla wars. The spirits of the Malaysian security forces are very good and the attempt to frighten them by mutilating the bodies of their comrades has not worked. If at all it has made our security personnel very angry and more determined to defeat the enemy. It has become almost a personal war for them. Malaysians must be thankful to our boys for their willingness to die for the country. It is not a *sandiwara* (stage play). It is real. The deaths and the wounding are real. If we are safe and secure, if we are stable and free from fear of guerrilla attacks, it is because our soldiers and police are ready to die for us.

Chedet.cc blog, 2013

ON TERRORISM

Killings, kidnappings and blackmail are not only committed by criminals but by countries as well. That these things often affect innocent people makes no difference. There are countries which try to assassinate certain people by bombing their residences. At the same time, they criticise the terrorists and acts of terrorism. *UMNO General Assembly, Kuala Lumpur, 1987*

৵

Conventional wars can be fought between sovereign nations no matter their relative sizes. But conventional wars failed as Arab nations tried to dislodge the Israelis. The only way for the Arabs to fight against what they perceive as gross injustice was to resort to guerilla warfare. Throughout the ages the Europeans have demonstrated innovativeness in warfare. Terrorist methods which involve putting innocent people at risk and killing them are largely European inventions. Some of these terroristic acts are state-initiatied.

International Conference of Religious Studies, Kuala Lumpur, 1999

৵

In the 1960s and early 1970s terrorists gangs abounded in Europe. The Baader-Meinhof gang was one of them. It was the Europeans who carried out the first hijacking of a commercial plane. In Northern Ireland bombs were exploded in the cities, killing men, women and children. The Arabs soon learnt the methods of terrorism as they sought to regain Palestine. They hijacked planes, they bombed buildings and they rampaged with blazing guns against everyone, their own people largely but also against the hated Europeans. There is no doubt that their methods were those of terrorists. But whereas others were called just terrorists, the Arabs were labelled Muslim terrorists. It is known that a few of the Arab terrorists were Christians but the label 'Muslim terrorists' was still stuck to them.

International Conference of Religious Studies, Kuala Lumpur, 1999

Terrorists have been with us throughout history. Over the last half a century, the terrorists have become more sophisticated and are much more focused. We may not agree with them, we may consider them misguided but it would be a mistake to think that they terrorise for the sake of terrorism, or because they enjoy terrorising their victims. Their evil deeds have a purpose, to them at least. They would not have willingly killed themselves in the most horrible fashion on September 11 if it was not because they believed there was a purpose for their suicide. *Conference on Terrorism, Kuala Lumpur, 2001*

≥●

We have to determine who is a terrorist. This is important because people who some people describe as terrorists are regarded as noble freedom fighters by some others. More confusing still, some are condemned as terrorists one day, only to be considered respectable people another day. If we want the whole world to join in the fight against terrorists, then we must ensure that a terrorist is a terrorist to all and everyone at all times. The Irish Republican Army is a terrorist organisation in the eyes of the British but are regarded as freedom fighters worthy of financial support by the Americans.

Conference on Terrorism, Kuala Lumpur, 2001

≥●

Malaysia is familiar with terrorism and the war against terrorists. Rebel-trained guerrillas believe that guerrillas can never be defeated. By their books the terrorists in Malaysia could not be defeated. But we defeated them. After fighting for 42 years, 1948 to 1990, the terrorists in Malaysia decided to lay down arms. *Conference on Terrorism, Kuala Lumpur, 2001*

≥●

The world is in a state of terror. We are quite paranoid. We are afraid of flying, of going to certain countries, fearful of certain people. We are afraid of white powder, shoes, metal cutlery on aircrafts. Recently in Australia an airport was evacuated because of the strong smell of a delicious Malaysian fruit. We are afraid of Muslims, of Arabs, of bearded people. We are afraid of war, of the disruption it can cause and the uncertainties.

Opening of the Non-Aligned Movement's Business South–South Cooperation Kuala Lumpur, 2003

The people who kidnap workers of various races and [kill them] by beheading them must be condemned. That they are not members of regular forces of government is no excuse. But when members of a government's disciplined force commit atrocities, torturing and killing prisoners, they must be considered worse than the irregular forces of extremist groups. They are the real terrosists.   *Cairo University, 2005*

કુ

If they choose to make every Muslim a terror suspect, they will have to accept that they have 1.6 billion enemies lurking in every corner of the world. But if they choose to eliminate the primary cause of the present violence and indiscriminate killings, then there is a good chance that the world will become secure again, that they can go anywhere in the world without fear of being blown up, kidnapped or simply being shot. Some might think this would be giving in to blackmail. Well, conventional war attacking a country is also blackmail. Give in or be killed and destroyed. Give in or the mailed fist would keep on hammering you. That is blackmail too. And you will pay the price for ignoring it.   *Stability and Justice and Rights of Al-Quds and Palestine, Kuala Lumpur, 2010*

કુ

The war against terror initiated by the United States has resulted in blockades against many Muslim oil-producing countries. In total disregard for international law and the United Nations, the United States is currently blockading Iran, a major oil exporter. In order to make the sanctions effective, the United States needs other countries to do the same. But countries which source their oil from Iran are naturally unwilling to join in the blockade. To get them to apply sanctions, the United States is now doing a lot of arm-twisting, making threats against the total trade of these countries. Countries like Malaysia are very susceptible. This great advocate of free trade, of globalisation, of a borderless world seems ever ready to renege on its undertaking on free trade. You get to trade freely if you do as you are told. But the United States cannot force China, Russia and India. No attempt is made against European countries either, because without Iranian oil their economies would grind to a stop. This great country which is so dedicated to promoting free trade picks and chooses the countries to bully.

Chedet.cc blog, 2012

ON THE UNITED NATIONS

When the United Nations was formed in 1945, the world felt that an agency had been found for the resolution of conflicts between nations. The failure of the League of Nations was forgotten in the euphoria that greeted the emergence of the United Nations Organisation. In the colonised territories like the states of the Malay Peninsula, hope was kindled that freedom and dignity were once again attainable. Such were the expectations in Malaysia that the most popular political party among the Malays, which today governs Malaysia as part of a coalition, was named after the United Nations Organisation. The United Malays National Organisation, of which I am the current president, drew a lot of inspiration and saw a lot of similarities between the Malay States and the United Nations as a concept.

Asia Society and Council of Foreign Relations, New York, 1982

The need to restore faith in the United Nations is very pressing. The United Nations must regain its credibility. I would like to say that countries like Malaysia must help restore the trust and confidence of the international community in this organisation's ability to play a constructive role in resolving problems and crises and in maintaining world peace and stability. But that would be pure rhetoric. What is needed is the full backing of the powerful nations. They must revitalise the organisation which they created. They must breathe life into it by abiding by its decisions and lending it their weight.

United Nations General Assembly, New York, 1982

We see the big powers continuing more and more to ignore and to belittle the United Nations. They have established a network of relationship outside the United Nations system to resolve world problems. They have formed their own economic clubs to which from time to time the developing countries are permitted to make their supplication. But the clubs – like all exclusive clubs – essentially look after the interest of its members.

United Nations General Assembly, New York, 1984

The United Nations, if it is to mean anything at all, must stand firm on principles, and there will be need for adjustments and compromise on the means, the processes, and the modalities. But there can be no compromise on principles. We, the smaller nations, cannot be blamed if we insist on that. It is hypocrisy to accuse us of being emotional or unrealistic, irresponsible or irrelevant only because those principles are now inconvenient to the major powers.

United Nations General Assembly, New York, 1984

The time for UN-bashing and the assault on multilateralism is over. If universal responsibility is a creed that this and future generations can believe in, then every country must provide full commitment to the United Nations. A revitalised United Nations poised to assume even greater responsibilities must not be hampered by a lack of financial resources. A *sine qua non* for its very survival is the timely payment by member countries of their assessed contributions.

United Nations General Assembly, New York, 1988

In contrast to the cynicism and the disillusionment that many have felt in the past about the UN, we are now witnessing a clear shift towards a better appreciation of the role of the UN and its relevance to the aspirations of the community of nations. We would like to believe that, at long last, the UN is coming into its own and fulfilling the tasks of moving conflicts from the battlefields to the conference table.

United Nations General Assembly, New York, 1988

Multilateralism had become a bad word as the powerful nations resorted to solving problems on their own. We are therefore pleased to welcome this change, this renewal of faith in the UN which we hope would mean the birth of a new era in multilateralism.

United Nations General Assembly, New York, 1988

As an international organisation, the UN must be perceived to be relevant in meeting the needs of its members, as a forum for multilateral diplomacy, as an instrument for maintaining international peace and security and as a catalyst for promoting international economic growth and development.

United Nations General Assembly, New York, 1988

ે

It is a matter of great assurance to all of us that the increased effectiveness of the Security Council has been made possible by the convergence of interest and action of the United States and the Soviet Union. Conversely it should be instructive to these two countries that they are drawing from the best of themselves when they counsel and collaborate together with the rest of the world on common objectives.

United Nations General Assembly, New York, 1988

ે

When one extols the achievements of the United Nations, one is not refusing to recognise that the steady improvement of relations between the United States and the Soviet Union have helped significantly in bringing about progress on conflict resolutions. All of us who have lived under periods of unease and uncertainty, when the two powers stared at each other eye-ball to eye-ball, are greatly relieved that these two superpowers are realistically discussing peace and construction between them.

United Nations General Assembly, New York, 1988

ે

For the UN to remain effective and dynamic, its strengths and weaknesses would have to be reviewed. Where necessary, organisational changes should be made to benefit all members and the world in general. The veto power accorded to the permanent members of the Security Council should be re-examined and the Security Council membership should also be expanded to take into account present realities. The credibility of the United Nations is at its lowest ebb. Unless it is more resolute, it will turn into a welfare body distributing aid after the event.

Dinner with New Zealand Prime Minister James Bolger, Kuala Lumpur, 1994

We see among others, endless carnage in Afghanistan, brutal and senseless massacre in Rwanda and savage aggression perpetrated by the Serbs in Bosnia-Herzegovina. All these situations call for decisive action by the Security Council. New Zealand's decision to provide more troops for peacekeeping in Bosnia-Herzegovina is most welcomed. Malaysia is also doing her part within her means. We will continue to uphold the principles of justice and fairplay. The blatant Serb aggression must not be allowed to continue in Bosnia-Herzegovina. The Security Council should take steps to lift sanctions so as to allow the Bosnians to defend themselves against Serb aggression. Peacekeepers are useless if they retreat when faced with defiance. If they are not prepared to take risks, they should allow their wards to defend themselves. Under no circumstance is it justified for them to sacrifice those they are supposed to protect in order to save their own skin.

Dinner with New Zealand Prime Minister James Bolger, Kuala Lumpur, 1994

The League of Nations had failed and the United Nations has not performed much better. The strong will dominate and the weak must submit. It is still a world of 'might is right'.   *Asia Pacific Parliamentary Forum, Kuala Lumpur, 2003*

ON APARTHEID

My government abhors South Africa's inhuman policy of apartheid. This is a travesty of justice and is an affront to human dignity. Apartheid, coupled with the Pretoria regime's deliberate and provocative armed incursions into neighbouring states, constitutes a major cause of tension and instability, not only in Africa, but also the world at large. Malaysia will continue to fully support the cause of the oppressed people of South Africa in their struggle for equality, justice and dignity against apartheid. Those who champion human rights, or claim to do so, could do better by condemning the Pretoria regime and treating them like the freaks that they are.

United Nations General Assembly, New York, 1982

ε

Malaysia does not trade with South Africa. We deprive ourselves of substantial revenue by so doing. But those whose application of sanctions are likely to bring South Africa to its knees, have any number of arguments why they should not apply sanctions. Restrictions on imports from poor countries, restrictions which cause real human sufferings in these small states are alright. But not sanctions against South Africa. The blacks would suffer. That is the excuse. The fact is that the blacks are already suffering. Cures are always painful. As a doctor, I should know. But to perpetuate sufferings is a poor alternative to the temporary pain of a cure. If sanctions can help destroy a despicable policy like apartheid, then sanctions must be applied and they must be applied by those who can hurt most; by the countries with the biggest economic clout. Failure to do so would mean hypocrisy on the part of these countries. And that will rub off on the Commonwealth.

Commonwealth Heads of Government Meeting, Nassau, Bahamas, 1985

ε

For some the fight for independence is not over yet. The blacks of South Africa are being hounded and hunted in order to sustain the most despicable system ever invented by man: apartheid.

Opening of the South–South II Conference, Kuala Lumpur, 1986

The South African government remains the most blatantly racialist regime in the history of the world. That it can exist in this day and age is due in part to the support it gets from its sympathisers in the North. People who are prepared to take direct military action against a government for allegedly promoting terrorism, advocate gentle persuasion when dealing with the open terrorism practised by the South African government. We do not expect the Pretoria regime to be bombed out of existence, because we do not believe in such a line of action. But when will those with the economic clout apply sanctions? Or is it that African lives are cheap, and that investments in South Africa are too profitable?

Opening of the South–South II Conference, Kuala Lumpur, 1986

ॐ

Malaysia holds the view that the Commonwealth is still a useful forum although, personally, I feel that it has not risen to the occasion when it is most needed. I refer to the despicable policy of apartheid practised by the white regime in South Africa. Malaysia applied sanctions unilaterally against South Africa since 1965 and we have lost billions of dollars as a result. I cannot believe that any British prime minister would want to see apartheid perpetuated. Yet Britain is unwilling to apply sanctions in the belief that it will do the blacks more harm than good. I don't think so. Indeed, I feel that, more than any other member of the Commonwealth, Britain has a moral duty to join the majority to bring about the end of minority rule and apartheid in South Africa.

Dinner in honour of Singapore Prime Minister Goh Chok Tong, Kuala Lumpur, 1987

ॐ

Many of the world's problems are still with us and among them is the despicable apartheid system of South Africa. The efforts to eliminate the hideous system and bring about majority rule in South Africa must be redoubled.   *Non-Aligned Movement, Belgrade, Yugoslavia, 1989*

ॐ

The white regime of South Africa must be ostracised and condemned. Sanctions must be more effectively applied.

Non-Aligned Movement, Belgrade, Yugoslavia, 1989

ON ASEAN

Given the will of all concerned, we may at this conference lay the foundation stones for the 'Pyramids of ASEAN'. Even though these ASEAN business pyramids may not achieve the status of being one of the wonders of the world, let us all at least try to establish these as fine examples of international economic cooperation.

Inauguration of ASEAN–West Asian Investment Conference, Kuala Lumpur, 1978

We in ASEAN firmly believe in regional cooperation as a means to achieve greater prosperity and stability for our region. It is with this belief that we have nurtured ASEAN.

Official Opening of ASEAN Travel Forum, Genting Highlands, 1981

Under the present Malaysian leadership, ASEAN will continue to feature prominently in Malaysia's foreign policy considerations. Since its inception in 1967, ASEAN has gained tremendous momentum and respect so much so it is recognised today as a regional entity and force in all matters pertaining to the region and indeed the world. Despite early scepticism, ASEAN has proven to the world to be a viable and cohesive grouping.   *Singapore, 1981*

In so far as Malaysia is concerned, ASEAN remains in the forefront of our foreign policy priorities. The rationale behind this government's thinking in this regard is the vital role of ASEAN as a stabilising influence and as a catalyst in developing the economic resilience of the region. We cannot prosper alone in a region that is in turmoil and unstable. To prosper, we have to have the kind of regional environment that is conducive to economic growth. Malaysia's adherence to the principles of ASEAN cooperation is therefore not altruistic. It is enlightened self-interest. And because it is so, we will always place the interest of ASEAN as a top priority.

Meeting of ASEAN Economic Ministers, Kuala Lumpur, 1982

It can thus be seen that suddenly five historically separated countries found themselves having to conduct relations not as familiar neighbours but as suspicious strangers. It would be a miracle if they do not mess up their relations. And, indeed, this was what happended initially. Within a very short space of time, they were in confrontation. Territorial claims were made and threats uttered. At one stage, the Sukarno regime [in Indonesia] actually dropped paratroopers on Malaysian territory.

Asia Society and Council of Foreign Relations, New York, 1982

ॐ

Local business people entertain different ideas. The ASEAN member with a small domestic market like Singapore would like to remove tariff barriers. But the Indonesian businessmen and the government would like to retain the potential of a 150 million population for themselves. So would Thailand and the Philippines, each with a population of about 45 million. Malaysia is neither here nor there. With a population of only 14+ million, it still manages to have the biggest passenger car market among the ASEAN five. It is comparatively a more affluent market.

Asia Society and Council of Foreign Relations, New York, 1982

ॐ

Among the kind of cooperation that is designed by ASEAN to ward off threats is the concept of a Zone of Peace, Freedom and Neutrality or ZOPFAN. This concept requires the cooperation of the big powers. That cooperation is not really forthcoming, but each of the big powers is not willing to say that they disapprove of peace or of freedom or of neutrality in Southeast Asia. In a sort of negative way, ZOPFAN is working.

Asia Society and Council of Foreign Relations, New York, 1982

ॐ

In the case of ASEAN, it can be said that regional grouping has had positive results in terms of economic cooperation itself. It depends more upon the willingness to know and understand each other and, accepting the shortcomings, to work within the constraints. No grand design should be tried purely because it sounds good or it had worked elsewhere.

Asia Society and Council of Foreign Relations, New York, 1982

Whatever has developed to date in respect of ASEAN is merely the tip of the iceberg. Whatever you see as potential for today is only a small fraction of the future potential that this region will offer to manufacturers who have the vision and the faith to see the progress of ASEAN and to take advantage of what we have to offer now.

ASEAN–EEC Industrial Sectoral Conference, Kuala Lumpur, 1983

ಶಿ

Many have said that the economic concepts within ASEAN are progressing very slowly. We say that we are progressing with 'deliberate speed'. We want to build a structure, brick by brick, so that the final edifice will stand the test of time. We do not want to act in haste just to satisfy our ego that we have got a great economic grouping, only to regret at leisure when we find the structure falling apart at the slightest stress. I must admit that we have learnt a lot from the EEC itself in terms of mistakes to avoid, and paths to pursue or not to pursue, and thus we will continue to 'make haste' cautiously. However, I would like to caution all potential investors not to be lulled into a sense of complacency because of the speed the various regional economic activities within ASEAN are progressing. The leaders of the ASEAN nations have committed themselves to policies and measures of economic co-operation designed to mutually lift the entire level of economic development within ASEAN.

ASEAN–EEC Industrial Sectoral Conference, Kuala Lumpur, 1983

ಶಿ

We most certainly do not want to continue to be the plantations and mines for Europe or the rest of the world. We most certainly do not cherish the dubious honour that ASEAN holds as a world leader in the production of various raw commodities whose prices are often dictated by the tender mercies of market manipulators and close-shop trading systems in Europe and other parts of the world. We most certainly do not want to see our peoples breaking their backs to till the soil and mine the land for depleting commodities, only to find that those who work the hardest are those who obtain the least economic benefits for their endeavours. Finally, we most certainly do not want to perpetuate our manufacturing sectors at the lower ranges of the scale of world technology.

ASEAN–EEC Industrial Sectoral Conference, Kuala Lumpur, 1983

Today we can be proud that ASEAN has made considerable progress as a regional grouping. Internationally, ASEAN has attained political prominence and credibility. Within the member countries themselves ASEAN consciousness is palpable. Our political cooperation and common stand on many international issues are expected and accepted by the international community and we have gained considerably by this. It is no coincidence that the member countries of ASEAN are politically stable and that the region has consistently registered economic growth well above world average.

Meeting of ASEAN Economic Ministers, Kuala Lumpur, 1985

ક

In a creative act of regional reconciliation, the ASEAN Five decided to create a different world for themselves. What exists today is a community, now expanded to six nations, where there is securely in place a structure of understanding and trust, goodwill and active cooperation unprecedented in the history of Southeast Asia. There were many obstacles in the way and more than just hiccups. But what we have now firmly established is a Pax Aseana, the more remarkable because it is a peace without an imperium. It might also be noted that the ASEAN community constitutes three quarters of Southeast Asian real estate. It is where three out of four Southeast Asians live and where more than nine-tenths of Southeast Asian income is generated.

Asia-Pacific Roundtable, Kuala Lumpur, 1989

ક

We must not be at sixes and threes. The mountain of distrust and misunderstanding must be removed. A divided Southeast Asia is not in the interest of any regional state. It is in the interest of all of Southeast Asia that we secure a healthy balance of forces, a system open to the world, composed of states which are economically prosperous, socially dynamic, strategically secure, domestically at peace and politically at one.

Asia-Pacific Roundtable, Kuala Lumpur, 1989

At this crucial turning point, the course that the states of ASEAN must take cannot just be to let others shape that history. We cannot be mere objects of international relations. With the 'East' in turmoil, the 'South' in continuing crisis, and the 'West' on an economic collision course, an active ASEAN can contribute positively. It is incumbent upon us to play a productive role in the making of the new international economic order. We must of course be aware of our limited weight in the international arena. There is every reason for humility. But the corruption arising from a sense of powerlessness is as bad as the corruption of power.

International Conference on the ASEAN Countries and the World Economy, Bali, 1991

ટ્રે

The ASEAN experience has shown that neighbouring countries can learn a lot from each other and can help each other to develop. When neighbours develop together, their intra-regional economic activities are enhanced for the benefit of all. Poor neighbours create problems particularly in terms of migration. Their markets too cannot contribute towards regional trade. Poor neighbours will consequently stunt regional growth.

Santiago, Chile, 1991

ટ્રે

I am also an Aseanist. Far too many ignorant people today underestimate ASEAN. It has been central to our post-colonial past. It will remain central to our future. Indeed, I confess, without any sense of guilt, that I will fight every impulse, contain every force and confront any danger that will damage or destroy the ASEAN family. For this, I make no apology. I express no reservation.

Opening of International General Meeting of the Pacific Economic Cooperation Council,
Kuala Lumpur, 1994

ટ્રે

When I first took over [as prime minister], I decided to review and change our foreign policy. I felt we should ignore ideological differences and be friendly with everyone. My first priority was building stronger relationships with the member countries of ASEAN as they were our close neighbours, and whatever happened to them would affect us.   *A Doctor In The House, 2011*

ON ASIA

Another common Asian practice is to give life-time employment in exchange for loyalty to the business entity concerned. But ethnic Europeans believe in dismissing employees whenever businesses is bad. The employees have to be taken care of by the government through unemployment benefits. This is the safety net that Western sociologists boast about. Their people consider this as their right, as their entitlement. As a result a large number of workers prefer not to work, but to be on unemployment allowance instead.

Prime Ministerial Lecture of Harvard Club, Kuala Lumpur, 1998

But contrary to those who seek the holy grail – the single model, the simple path, the one standard formula, the one 'secret' – of Asia's success, I believe that the various Asian societies have been inventing and re-inventing themselves according to different formulas at different times. We have achieved whatever we have achieved according to the Sinatra Principle. We have all done it our own way.

World Economic Forum, Singapore, 1999

Please do not assume that we in Asia are always stupid. I must admit that many of us are indeed stupid, incredibly stupid sometimes. If I were to list all the stupid things I have done, it would take all day. But please do give us a little credit. We can be stupid some of the time. We can be stupid a lot of the time. But please do not expect us to be stupid all the time. If you do not understand some of the apparently stupid things we have done, you might now and again do well to do a little more work and improve your ability to understand, rather than to assume that we are just stupid.

World Economic Forum, Singapore, 1999

There is a tendency in this part of Asia to think that East Asia is Asia, and that South Asia, Central Asia and West Asia do not count. Of course Russian Asia is totally ignored. But in talking about Asia, its present and its future, these other very substantial parts of Asia must be taken into account. Maybe we don't think anything much would happen in these parts which would be as dynamic as in East Asia, but it is entirely possible that these parts of Asia would change too. Already India is showing signs of economic dynamism.

Asia Society Gala Forum, Hong Kong, 2000

૨▲

The picture of Asia at the beginning of the new millennium. It is a dismal picture. Much of the energy and the spirit which had driven it in the past has been dissipated. No Genghis Khan, Akhbar the Great, no Mongol or Turkish hordes are likely to appear on the scene. Because of its extreme diversity and the distances which separate its people, Asians cannot come together the way the Europeans can come together.   Asia Society Gala Forum, Hong Kong, 2000

૨▲

Asia must accept that it is a divided continent. Accepting this, it must plan its future as separate sub-continents, growing according to its special comparative advantages and at different paces.

Asia Society Gala Forum, Hong Kong, 2000

૨▲

Asians everywhere must have pride in their values and culture and their ways of managing their countries and their problems. The attempts by the West to force their values and ideologies on Asians must be resisted. Remember that Communism and Socialism were invented by the West and these two ideologies have retarded the development of so many countries which adopted them, countries in Asia and Africa. There is no reason why we should believe that what is being propagated by the West now – liberal democracy, free markets, borderless world, etc., would do any better in the long run.

Asia Society Gala Forum, Hong Kong, 2000

It is not so in Asia. The area is so vast that delineation of boundaries was not easy. Though there are distinct ethnic groups, but most Asians are sub-divided into tribes which off and on came together under strong tribal leaders. Thus the Seljuks, the Ottomans, the Mongols and the Manchus. Asians built empires in Asia largely but these empires were not durable. The death of a powerful leader invariably led to a break-up into numerous little empires or states. By the beginning of the 20th century, almost all the Asian countries had come under the rule of various European powers, including the European Russians who subjugated the Central Asians. Almost without exception the Asian countries under European domination remained backward and poor. The only country which managed to remain independent and to industrialise along the European pattern was Japan.

Asia Society Gala Forum, Hong Kong, 2000

&

Asia today is in total disarray. West Asia continues to be unstable as they glare at each other and undermine each other. Rich in oil and other resources, they are nevertheless underdeveloped. They have no country with an industrial economy capable of supplying even their own needs. They are totally dependent on the developed countries of the West, and many are subservient to the Western powers. *Asia Society Gala Forum, Hong Kong, 2000*

&

Any idea about Asia dominating the world in the 21st century should be abandoned. It is not feasible and it will merely serve to antagonise the rest of the world, in particular the European nation on both sides of the Atlantic. Neither should any Asian nation harbour ideas about dominating Asia. Asia and Asian nations must be free, truly free. No one should impose their values or ideologies or system on Asia. While everyone should be concerned over human rights, the environment, etc., no one from within or outside Asia should appoint himself or his country as the policeman charging himself with the responsibility to ensure that everyone behaves. Asian countries are mature enough to know what is right and what is wrong.

Asia Society Gala Forum, Hong Kong, 2000

We must know that civilisation began in Asia. When the ethnic Europeans were still clothed in animal skin, Asians were already ruling vast areas under complex government systems. Asian leaders promoted knowledge acquisition and the arts, built and led great nations and empires. But today Asian leaders wait to be led. We ask permission from the ethnic Europeans whether we should talk to each other. When the East Asian Economic Caucus was proposed as a logical move following the setting up of the European Union and NAFTA [North American Free Trade Agreement], we meekly waited for the official approval of the Americans. Even now we dare not call ourselves East Asian Economic whatever. Instead we hide behind the ASEAN+3.

Ho Rih Hwa Public Lecture Series, Singapore, 2004

ăạ

Asians have always believed in the role of government in regulating institutions. The world is about to view Asian practices and systems more positively. Asian countries must therefore make their voices heard. And this includes the small developing economies as well. It would be fatal for them if they allow, as in the past, the rich and the powerful to devise the systems by which they must all function. In particular the banking system and practices need to be looked at from the Asian developing economies' point of view and interest. But that culture, that blind acceptance of the systems and ways of the Europeans, must be modified, if not discarded. What we are seeing today is the collapse of a very fundamental European institution, that of money and banking.   *Annual Top Executive Forum on Governance, Bali, 2008*

ăạ

Asians are culturally conservative and orthodox. They prefer to do things the way they had done in the past. But Asians also have an inferiority complex and believe that the Europeans are superior people with brilliant ideas and ways of doing things. The Asians subscribe to the Eurocentric world and would always try to emulate the Europeans.

Annual Top Executive Forum on Governance, Bali, 2008

ON THE MEDIA

We in Malaysia are particularly concerned with the frequent incidents of misreporting, deliberate or otherwise, about our affairs in the foreign press, especially Western press. We had our first few bitter doses of uncalled-for publicity shortly after the May 13, 1969 racial riots in which foreign readers were regaled with distorted views of the events happening then. Indeed dire predictions were made which implied that the world could write off Malaysia. In the event Malaysia did not only get over her difficulties, but she emerged stronger, more united and more prosperous than ever before.

Opening of the General Assembly of the Organisation of Asian News Agencies,
Kuala Lumpur, 1981

A trend that is to be applauded is investigative reporting. Unfortunately, only a thin invisible line separates investigative reporting from muck-raking. The world must have secrets which should not be exposed if relationship between nations is to be good. If every single thought about our friends are known to them, they will not remain friends. So, while investigative reporting is good, we should be careful not to allow such reports to degenerate into muck-raking.

Opening of the General Assembly of the Organisation of Asian News Agencies,
Kuala Lumpur, 1981

It is my hope that the time would not be too long for us to see Asia's image being painted by Asians themselves rather than by outsiders who are neither sensitive to our needs and aspirations nor sympathetic to our cause. A just and equitable distribution of information within the region and outside it would inevitably help promote regional understanding and, in the long run, enhance further the co-operative efforts among the countries of the region.

Opening of the General Assembly of the Organisation of Asian News Agencies,
Kuala Lumpur, 1981

The Western-controlled international media have subverted the governments of many developing countries until some are overthrown. The sad thing is that the governments which took over are often less democratic than the maligned predecessor. Whatever governments take over, they soon become subjects of international vilification by the western media.

Opening of the General Assembly of the Organisation of Asian News Agencies,
Kuala Lumpur, 1981

છે

I have no negative assessments about the curbing of press freedom in Britain and the United States, through the introduction of censorship, during the First and Second World Wars – although I do believe that it is important to remind some of the more fervent but blind preachers what they did when the necessary had to be done.   *World Press Convention, Kuala Lumpur, 1985*

છે

If it is assumed that power tends to corrupt and absolute power tends to corrupt absolutely, by what magical formula is the media itself, with all its awesome power, exempt from this inexorable tendency? Is power the only cause of corruption? Freedom too can corrupt and absolute freedom can corrupt absolutely.   *World Press Convention, Kuala Lumpur, 1985*

છે

Having caused so much offense thus far, let me now tilt at the towering windmill of the Western media whose power over the minds of the entire world is so massive and so utterly pervasive. As a Third Worlder I ask: Why must this entire planet be seen from the Western, Orientalist perspective? Why must the Third World be judged day in and day out only according to the self-righteous values of the West and its media? Why must so much sheer arrogance and sheer ignorance wreak so much havoc on the Third World? Is freedom of the press, a value which I have been taught to treasure, nothing more than the right of a few editors and a few owners to censor and to decide what we all should read, listen to and watch?   *Trinity College, Oxford, 1985*

Certain quarters bemoan the lack of press freedom and maintain that rumours are necessary as the newspapers, they claim, print only government propaganda. These quarters are not only quoted by the local press, but their views are sought and published on any and every issue. None of their views are supportive of the government. Some even create racial and economic problems. But they get published anyway in this country where there is supposed to be no press freedom. Only the most blatantly provocative and damaging views attract the kind of punitive section they say the government doles out lavishly.

EMF Foundation Round Table, Kuala Lumpur, 1986

Newspeople do not like countries that are calm and peaceful and attains economic growth as a matter of course. Politically, too, there is not much to report about Malaysia. Since independence in 1957 it has been ruled by coalition governments which, despite frequent admission of new members, keep and practise consistent policies, particularly towards foreign investors. Recently, as you know, the same coalition won with a four-fifths majority, which also means a mandate to continue with well-tried policies. Like Holiday Inn, no surprises. No sudden 180° or even 90° turns.

American International Group Investment Seminar, Kuala Lumpur, 1986

Absolute freedom does not exist, as freedom must always be limited by certain requirements of the society or even the environment. The same rule applies to the media whereby freedom of the media is not absolute.

Perdana Discourse Series 6, Perdana Leadership Foundation, Putrajaya, 2007

If you read foreign press reports about Malaysia, even if they are talking about something else, they never fail to mention Malaysia where the press is controlled.

Perdana Discourse Series 6, Perdana Leadership Foundation, Putrajaya, 2007

We cannot deny that the press is controlled. But, again, control is something that can be used either in a good way or a bad way. Some controls are good, I think our currency control yielded good results, but some controls are bad.

Perdana Discourse Series 6, Perdana Leadership Foundation, Putrajaya, 2007

૨&

I was once advised to have a spin doctor because Mr Blair had a spin doctor when he was elected as the prime minister of Britain. A friend of mine in England wrote to me and said that I should have spin doctors. But I have a habit of doing things myself and shooting my mouth, so I do not think that spin doctors will do me any good because they might say something and I might go off and say something else. Therefore, I decided not to have spin doctors.

Perdana Discourse Series 6, Perdana Leadership Foundation, Putrajaya, 2007

૨&

The media must of course be conscious of its responsibility and its role. The media however is also influenced by other things like making money. Certain people have invested in the media and want to make money out of it.

Perdana Discourse Series 6, Perdana Leadership Foundation, Putrajaya, 2007

૨&

The world is in a bad shape because politicians instead of journalists run it. I came to this conclusion after reading a copy of *The Economist*, the British magazine. The writers in *The Economist* seem to know everything that ails the world and they also know how all these ailments can be cured.

Chedet.cc blog, 2013

ON HIMSELF AND FAMILY

As a doctor, one is always tempted to look at problems as diseases, and the people affected by them as patients. Since taking up politics and the chores of running a government, that temptation has seldom been resisted by me, and I must admit the clinical approach to problems pays. In the case of promoting investments, investors and patients are very apt. Patients are never satisfied with what they have, and this has driven more doctors round the bend than the income tax they have to pay.

Conference on Business in Southeast Asia, Kuala Lumpur, 1977

ॐ

Not being an economist or a financial expert, I always feel inadequate when dealing with this subject. I am sure you will find me quite naive. But being a politician, the only profession that needs no diplomas or degrees, the idea of speechifying is always irresistable. Even if one may sound absurd, one feels that an opportunity to speak must not be allowed to pass.

Annual Dinner of Financial Institutions, Kuala Lumpur, 1990

ॐ

Since I am without formal training in economics and finance, I have to fall back on the oldest logical approach to understanding a subject or problem, i.e. by *reductio ad absurdum*. It has always proven, at least to me, a formidable weapon of logic and almost never fails. It is a means of reducing things to basics in order to understand and to extrapolate from there. There is a saying in Malay, 'Jika sesat jalan, balik ke pangkal' – if you are lost, return to the beginning. My economics is consequently very basic and I hope you will excuse me if sometimes I state the obvious as if it is some new-found and original discovery. *Annual Dinner of Financial Institutions, Kuala Lumpur, 1990*

I would like to thank the organisers, the Cambridge University Malaysia Society (CUMAS), for inviting me to this conference on 'Malaysia in the New Millennium'. I hope that some of the glory of this centre of learning will rub off on me, as I could never aspire to be a graduate of Cambridge with the coveted B.A. Cantab.

Malaysia in the New Millenium Conference, London, 2000

❧

Please let me apologise for not being hypocritical and for not saying some of the things that some may wish me to say. I am tempted to try but as a medical doctor I am a little worried about the effects of a physiological process called 'choking'. I am sure you would not want me to choke on my words and to collapse right before your very eyes.

World Economic Development Congress, Kuala Lumpur, 2001

❧

I don't believe in saying nice things, I rather say what I feel and deal with it.

World Economic Forum, Davos, Switzerland, 2003

❧

When I went to the medical college, I was among those with the least qualifications. All the other boys, the boys from Singapore and Malaysia, they all went to medical college with at least six distinctions. Six, seven, eight distinctions. They were all brilliant. I had only three distinctions, and that was the highest among the Malay boys. So I was the brilliant – in, you know, in a small pond, you feel big. But when you enlarge the pond, you feel you're small. You see, among the Malays, I was the best. But when mixed up with all these Chinese and Indian boys, I felt very small indeed. And they told me actually, to pack my bags and go home. Because the medical course is not for me, really. With three distinctions what can you do?

Perdana Discourse Series 3, Perdana Leadership Foundation, Putrajaya, 2005

I remember when I took my pathology examination. I read the [pathology] book – I don't know how many times – so much so, when I was answering the questions, I could actually see the page that was relevant to that question. I could practically read the page and see the illustration. So it was easy for me to just extract from what I saw, which was already in my mind. So when you do it repeatedly, it is possible for you, without any effort really – not trying to memorise, I didn't try to memorise. But I looked at the page, I read the page over and over again until, somehow or other it became a picture in my mind. *Perdana Discourse Series 3, Perdana Leadership Foundation, Putrajaya, 2005*

❧

Do everything repeatedly. Even if it is manual work, it's the same. I, as you know, I dabble with wood carving. All the wood carvings I do, the first one looks horrible. The second one is better, the third one is even better. Eventually, after doing it many, many times, I get the things right. I carved an aeroplane, for example, not a very difficult thing. Using the wood-turning machine we can have the body, and then it's a matter of carving the rest. And eventually I did get a good model aeroplane. *Perdana Discourse Series 3, Perdana Leadership Foundation, Putrajaya, 2005*

❧

Law can be used to perpetuate certain things such as the power of certain leaders. I do not know whether when I was a prime minister, I used such a provision to ensure that I stay in power for 22 years but I am quite sure that many people are quite confident that I did. But, my conscience is clear; if people want to oppose me, they may do so. *Perdana Discourse Series 6, Perdana Leadership Foundation, Putrajaya, 2007*

I remember some events in which I was involved, but only vaguely. If you ask me what did I do on August 12, 1982, or on any other day, I would not be able to tell you. Other people with the proverbial photographic memory can, but I cannot. I am quite certain if I ask the questioner what he did on any particular day in the times long past, he probably cannot tell me either. But then in a court or commission he or the judge or commissioners have the right to question, I had only the right to answer. This is very unsatisfactory. In a court of law, if you fail to remember every detail of what you did on a particular day 5, 10 or 15 years ago, then you must be lying, you must be hiding something. This possibility would be ominous – though it may not be ascertained with exactitude. But why bother about those niceties? Just conclude that a person who cannot remember is simply lying. I am going to take a memory course. Should I have occasion to be investigated or summoned to face a trial, I would be able to remember the suit I wore any day in my life and where I was when wearing the particular suit on a particular day. *Chedet.cc blog,* 2008

Going to school was thrilling to me and I couldn't wait for school holidays to end. I did fairly well and my Senior Cambridge Examinations result was good enough for me to be admitted into the medical faculty of the King Edward VII College of Medicine. I was given financial aid which was not a scholarship. The British colonial government apparently practised affirmative action because all my Chinese and Indian classmates had far better results than me. The examination results of the other six Malay students were even worse than mine. There were 70 plus students in all. I owed my teachers in school a great deal. Only one of them, Mr Zain, is alive today. He was a great teacher and spoke grammatically correct English all the time. Schooling was such a great experience and I recall with fondness many rewarding events that I went through. I hope and pray that all Malaysians remember their school days and the part that school plays in their lives. *Chedet.cc blog,* 2008

I admit that ever since I became minister of education in 1974, through my period as deputy prime minister and then 22 years as prime minister, I committed a lot of mistakes. I would not be human if I did not. I am sure my critics also made mistakes in their lifetime. The only difference is that their mistakes affected only themselves. But if they get the chance to be PM, maybe they will make the same mistakes I made. And we all will suffer. Now we are seeing the former opposition parties forming governments in several states. They were before very critical of government mistakes. Now they seem to be making mistakes too. Malaysians will have a tough time in the next general election. They may not like Barisan Nasional which for 50 years has been throwing tens of thousands into detention under the Internal Security Act, wasting public money building towers, airports, ports, highways, etc., muzzling the press, etc., etc. But they will find the so-called alternative coalition not much better. Really Malaysia is a most unfortunate country. It has experienced misrule ever since independence. And it looks like it will continue to be misruled whether the incumbent or the opposition wins. Maybe independence was a mistake also. How much better we would be under British rule. No one would be detained under the ISA. Everyone, communists included, would be able to speak their minds and contest in elections. Someone should be blamed for making the mistake of fighting for independence. *Chedet.cc blog*, 2009

The Western press launched a concerted effort to demonise the new prime minister [Dato' Sri Mohd Najib Tun Abdul Razak]. From France to Britain to Australia, the articles are identical and carried the same message. The incoming PM is said to be corrupt and involved in a murder case. The Australian writer says Malaysia is a 'pariah' nation. I cannot believe that this demonisation by so many at the same time is a coincidence. Included in the condemnation of the new PM is the allegation that he would bring back 'Mahathirism'. By this the Western press seem to imply that the fourth PM was a dictator who detained for no reason, manipulated the judiciary, controlled the press, etc., etc. As the person concerned, I will leave it to Malaysians to judge and to define 'Mahathirism'. They are the constituents which Najib should care about. The foreign press has an agenda of their own. *Chedet.cc blog*, 2009

Of course I don't like to be criticised. Anyone who says he likes criticism must be a hypocrite.

౭ఎ

I am not an intellectual but I admit that I use my brain more often than most. I was one with the lowest results in my Senior Cambridge Examination to be admitted in the College of Medicine. There were seven Malays whose results were all very inferior to the other students. Apparently the British were practising affirmative action in 1947. So much for being an intellectual. It did not need a very intelligent person to notice that Malays were generally poor as compared to others in the state of Kedah in the 1930s, 40s and 50s, the years when I was growing up in Alor Setar. They clearly faced a dilemma whether to get something of the wealth of their country for themselves or to just remain as they were. Hence the book *The Malay Dilemma*.

Chetdet.cc blog, 2012

౭ఎ

I am not a complex person. There is no mystery about what I did. If other PMs want to do what I did, they can. But if they have other agenda then they would attend to fulfilling their agenda. It is as simple as that. There really is no necessity to figure out the complexity of the thought process and the mystery of doing these simple things.

Chedet.cc blog, 2012

CHRONOLOGY

1925   Mahathir Mohamad born in Kedah

1941   Japan invades the Malay Peninsula and begins its four-year occupation

1946   UMNO is founded

Mahathir joins UMNO

1953   Mahathir graduates from King Edward VII College of Medicine, Singapore

1956   Mahathir marries Siti Hasmah Mohamad Ali

1957   Federation of Malaya achieves independence

1963   Malaysia is formed, comprising the Federation of Malaya, Sabah, Sarawak and Singapore

1964   Mahathir elected as a MP for Kota Setar Selatan, Kedah

1965   Singapore separates from Malaysia and becomes an independent republic

1969   May 13, 1969 racial riots

Mahathir loses his parliamentary seat in the general election

Mahathir expelled from UMNO for criticising its leadership

1970   *The Malay Dilemma* published

1971   New Economic Policy introduced

1973   Mahathir appointed senator

1974   Barisan Nasional officially registered with the Registrar of Societies

Mahathir resigns from Senate to re-enter politics

Mahathir rejoins UMNO

Mahathir elected as MP for Kubang Pasu, Kedah

Mahathir appointed minister of education

1975	Mahathir elected vice president of UMNO
1976	Mahathir appointed deputy prime minister
1978	Mahathir appointed minister of trade and industry
	Mahathir elected UMNO deputy president
1981	Mahathir appointed prime minister
	Mahathir becomes UMNO president
1985	Launch of the Proton Saga, the first Malaysian car
1987	High Court rules UMNO should be deregistered
	UMNO Baru formed and takes over the defunct party's organisational network and financial resources
1990	Vision 2020 articulated
	Mahathir elected chairman of G-15
1995	Official launch of Putrajaya, the nation's new administrative capital
1996	Launch of the Multimedia Super Corridor
1997	Asian Financial Crisis begins
1998	Mahathir introduces capital controls in response to the Asian Financial Crisis
	Malaysia hosts the Commonwealth Games
1999	Mahathir officially opens the world's tallest building, the Petronas Twin Towers
2003	Mahathir retires from the premiership after 22 years
	Mahathir conferred the title 'Tun' by the Yang di-Pertuan Agong
2007	Mahathir establishes the Kuala Lumpur War Crimes Commission
2008	Mahathir resigns from UMNO, citing a lack of confidence in the party's leadership
2009	Mahathir rejoins UMNO

ENDNOTES

1 National Front is the English translation of Barisan Nasional.

2 Lim Kit Siang, long-time leader of the Democratic Action Party.

3 Pakatan is the Malay term for pact or alliance.

4 Dadah is the Malay term for illegal drugs.

5 Ops Lalang (Operation Lalang) was undertaken by the Malaysian police on October 27, 1987 to prevent racial riots. More than 100 people were arrested under the Internal Security Act and the publishing licences of several newspapers revoked.

6 Bumiputera is the Malay term used to refer to ethnic Malays as well as other indigenous ethnic groups accorded special privileges under the Federal Constitution.

7 A chador is an outer garment worn by many Iranian women in public. It is a body-length semi-circle of fabric worn over the head and held clasped by the wearer at the front.

8 Sekolah Warisan is the Malay term for Vision School. Such schools were designed to comprise three schools (typically one Malay-medium, one Chinese-medium and one Tamil-medium) which would share the same compound and facilities while retaining separate school adminstrations.

9 Merdeka is the Malay expression used for independence.

10 Adat is Malay customary law.

11 The New Economic Policy was a government policy formulated in 1970 which aimed, over a 20-year period, to correct socioeconomic imbalances by eradicating poverty and reducing the correlation of race with economic function. It took the form of affirmative action to assist the Bumiputera within the context of an expanding economy.

12 The New Development Policy (1991–2000) built on the thrust of the NEP and continued to emphasise growth with equity.

13 The National Vision Policy was a government policy covering the years 2001–10. It incorporated past key development strategies and introduced new policy thrusts aiming to transform Malaysia into a knowledge-based society.

14 Vision 2020 was the plan, announced by Dr Mahathir in 1991, for Malaysia to achieve 'fully developed nation' status by the year 2020.

15 *Sogo shosha* are general trading companies unique to Japan.

16 Jamalul Kiram (1938–2013) was a claimant sultan of the Sultanate of Sulu.

PUBLISHER'S ACKNOWLEDGEMENTS

Most of the quotations in this book were selected from the resources of the Perdana Leadership Foundation's electronic research library. This invaluable online resource contains more than 320,000 digital records of speeches, news clippings, books and journal articles. Most of these materials can be accessed via http://library.perdana.org.my.

Editions Didier Millet is grateful to MPH Group Publishing for permission to use excerpts from *A Doctor in the House* by Dr Mahathir bin Mohamad, ISBN 9789675997228. The excerpts were 21b, 34c, 101a and 145d.

Editions Didier Millet is also grateful for the permission granted to use excerpts from *The Malay Dilemma* by Dr Mahathir bin Mohamad, ISBN 9789812616500, published by Marshall Cavendish International (Asia) Pte Ltd. The excerpts were 15a, 32a, 50a, 50b, 62a, 73a, 73b, 73c, 74a and 74b.

Lastly, we would like to thank Tun Dr Mahathir Mohamad for kindly agreeing to the publication of this anthology of quotations.